rustic fruit desserts

rustic fruit desserts

CRUMBLES, BUCKLES, COBBLERS, PANDOWDIES, AND MORE

Cory Schreiber and Julie Richardson
PHOTOGRAPHY BY Sara Remington

TEN SPEED PRESS
Berkeley | Toronto

Ten Speed Press
PO Box 7123
Berkeley, California 94707
www.tenspeed.com

Distributed in Australia by Simon and Schuster Australia, in Canada by Ten Speed Press Canada,
in New Zealand by Southern Publishers Group, in South Africa by Real Books, and in the United
Kingdom and Europe by Publishers Group UK.

Cover and text design by Nancy Austin
Food styling by Erin Quon
Prop styling by Kami Bremyer

A warm thank you to Hans Schoepflin for the use of his beautiful house to create this book,
and a large thank you to Alison Ghiorse at Savory Thymes for her assistance.

Library of Congress Cataloging-in-Publication Data

Schreiber, Cory, 1961–
  Rustic fruit desserts : crumbles, buckles, cobblers, pandowdies, and more / Cory Schreiber and
Julie Richardson ; photography by Sara Remington.
      p. cm.
  Includes index.
  Summary: "A collection of simple and satisfying recipes for crisps, slumps, buckles, grunts, and
other old-timey desserts by a beloved Portland bakery owner in collaboration with one of the region's
top chefs"—Provided by publisher.
  ISBN 978-1-58008-976-0
  1. Desserts. 2. Cookery (Fruit) I. Richardson, Julie, 1970– II. Title.
  TX773.S333 2009
  641.8'6—dc22
                            2008049349

Printed in China
First printing, 2009

1 2 3 4 5 6 7 8 9 10 — 13 12 11 10 09

For my wife, Joy,
who loves Marionberry pie. —CS

For my husband, Matt,
for suffering through the daily recipe
tastings and for bearing a few extra
pounds during the production
of this book. —JR

contents

fall

winter

pantry

acknowledgments

First and foremost, thank you to Julie Richardson, whose recipes are the foundation of this book. When Ten Speed Press approached me about this project, I knew Julie would be a wonderful and talented person to collaborate with, and our experience working together on this book has proven me right. I give Julie (as well as the charming staff at Baker & Spice and her supportive husband, Matt) much of the credit for *Rustic Fruit Desserts*.

I would also like to thank my friends at Ten Speed Press. I worked with Ten Speed ten years ago when I wrote my first cookbook, and writing this book has meant reconnecting with some old contacts and meeting new ones: Melissa Moore, Nancy Austin, Aaron Wehner, Phil Wood, Jasmine Star, and Sara Remington, thank you for all of your work on this book.

Finally, I would like to pay special tribute to all of the fruit growers who tend their orchards and crops with great care, cultivating sustained growth such that their farms continue to feed our communities and preserve our land. Without these dedicated individuals, this book would not be possible.

—*Cory Schreiber*

I enjoyed so many firsts over the course of writing this book. I am indebted to Cory Schreiber for the chance to even be part of such a project. Thank you, Cory, for having the faith in my ability to create the recipes you envisioned; it has been a true pleasure collaborating with you. To Joy Ellis, a thousand thanks for your humor and expertise (and the many late nights!) in tackling the recipes in their roughest form and translating them into desserts. Thanks for making me look so good.

My undying appreciation to the staff of Baker & Spice for allowing me the time away from the daily routine to work on this project and for reminding me that everything always runs smoothly in my absence. To my parents, for believing in me enough to invest in my dreams and for guiding me with your love and expertise.

Thanks to Lauren Holden for your insights, suggestions, and fantastic recipe testing. Many thanks to my recipe testing crew: Gina Fleschner, Stevey Conover, Nellie Hester, Phyliss Leonard, and Jo Newhouse. Thank you for fitting my crazy schedule into your baking lives.

Many thanks to all of the wonderful people at Ten Speed Press for the guidance, education, and understanding they have bestowed on me as a first-time author, with a special thanks to Melissa Moore. Thank you to Nancy Austin for your art of design and to Sara Remington for your beautiful photographs; you both truly know how to capture the elegance of fruit.

I have had the pleasure of working with or for so many creative and gifted bakers from whom I have gleaned much expertise. I have learned from reading many books by my baking heroes and from making a lot of mistakes of my own. Thank you to all of those who have shared with me your talents. I would not be the baker I am today without your willingness to contribute.

Finally, I share in Cory's commitment to the family farms of our land. Thank you for all of your hard work in tending to the fruits and berries that I had the pleasure to develop into *Rustic Fruit Desserts*.

—*Julie Richardson*

introduction

Cory's Perspective

I first met Julie Richardson at the Portland Farmers Market in 1998. Back then, she sold handcrafted baked goods at a small booth called Baker & Spice. A farmers market was the natural place for Julie to sell her pastries and pies, as she made them with seasonal, locally grown fruit. Her rustic desserts were deliciously irresistible, and I became far too familiar with almost all of them.

Given the devoted Baker & Spice following that lined up in droves every Saturday morning, rain or shine, (this is Portland, after all) to eat a breakfast pastry or buy a dessert to go, Baker & Spice eventually outgrew its farmers market booth. It now has a home as a retail bakery in the Hillsdale community of southwest Portland. Even though Baker & Spice is no longer at the farmers market, Julie's seasonal approach is still a mainstay of her baking. The bakery is committed to local foods and seasonal products, and its repertoire of classic fruit desserts, from pies and pandowdies to cobblers and crumbles, changes throughout the year to reflect the freshest fruits available.

In the Pacific Northwest, we are lucky to have a wide variety of seasonal fruits grown by small-scale farmers. This creates an abundance of delicious choices that can be baked into a vast selection of fruit desserts—much like the ones that keep customers queued up at Baker & Spice. No wonder Julie and her family have made Oregon their home! Julie grew up in rural Vermont, where orchards and berry fields were part of the summer landscape of her childhood. Turning fruit into dessert came naturally to her long before she engaged in professional baking.

This book combines Julie's knowledge of baking and my knowledge of Pacific Northwest fruits. I have cooked professionally for more than three decades, and at least half of my career has involved cooking in the Pacific Northwest. My most formative food memories are from Oregon, and I share Julie's passion for the quality of our fruit. I conjure up the seasons by thinking about various fruit desserts I have enjoyed: for autumn, it is a cobbler with blackberries bubbling in their juices beneath a golden cream biscuit; in the dead of winter, a comforting pear bread pudding made with brioche and lots of vanilla; for spring, a tart rhubarb compote over a scoop of vanilla ice cream; and for summer, a crunchy oatmeal crisp bursting with midsummer's sweet nectarines and raspberries.

Deciding what dessert to make on any given day is a wonderful process. You will find the dessert recipes in this book quite versatile, allowing you to take advantage of fruit at the peak of its season. Your decision of what to make could be based on the fruit you see at a local fruit stand or whatever fruit you have available in your kitchen. The ingredients in your pantry may also help dictate what form your dessert takes. And do not forget to consider how much time you have to prepare your dessert, so you can enjoy the process and not feel rushed.

Although I am familiar with the many varieties of fruit that grow in the Pacific Northwest, memorizing the differences between all the playfully named fruit desserts is beyond me. The desserts in this book fall into a number of categories, most of which are described below. Various regions of the United States have slightly different versions of these desserts, so my apologies if what I call a cobbler is what you call a slump, or vice versa.

A **pie** is a dessert with a filling (in this case, fruit) with a bottom crust and an optional top crust. Pies with both a bottom and a top crust are often referred to as a "double crust." Hand pies are a signature item at Baker & Spice; these individual pocket pies have pie filling in a flaky crust that is folded over and crimped shut.

Close relatives of the pie include the tart and the galette. A **tart** is a pie without a top crust; the fruit filling can be either fresh or cooked, and often it is coupled with another sweet, creamy filling. A **galette** is a rustic, free-form tart that does not require a pan.

A **cobbler** is a deep-dish fruit pie. It has a dense pastry on top (usually a sweet cream biscuit crust) and a fruit filling, with no crust beneath. In some versions, the crust completely covers the fruit, while other versions have a dropped-biscuit topping that leaves some fruit exposed.

A **grunt**, or **slump**, is more common in New England than in the Pacific Northwest. This dessert is similar to a cobbler but is usually cooked on top of the stove. In some parts of New England, it is a steamed pudding with berries.

A **crisp** or a **crumble** is a baked fruit dessert with a streusel topping. The crumb topping is traditionally made with butter, brown sugar, flour, and spices. Nuts and oats, and even bread crumbs and crushed cookies, can be added to the topping. The crumb topping is scattered over the fruit and usually melts into it.

A **betty** features fruit that is layered between or on top of diced bread cubes—anything from basic white bread to brioche to challah to day-old baguette. In some parts of the country, a betty is made like a crisp, only with buttered bread crumbs (and no nuts or oats) as the streusel.

A **pandowdy** is a deep-dish dessert that can be made with a variety of fruit. The topping is a crumbled biscuit, except the crust is broken up during the baking process and pushed down into the fruit to allow the juices to come through. Sometimes the crust is on the bottom and the dessert is inverted before serving.

A **buckle** has a cake batter poured in a single layer, with berries added to the batter. It is often made with blueberries because the berries sink yet keep their shape in the batter. Once baked, the cake has a "buckled" appearance. Think of a buckle as halfway between a cake and a fruit crisp. Buckles are great for breakfast!

A **teacake** is a simple cake akin to a coffee cake. Moist and tender, it can be eaten with one's fingers at tea time or any other time. Teacake packs well for picnics.

A **fool** is a simple summer dessert made of fruit at its peak layered with whipped cream.

A **trifle** is a visually stunning dessert made by layering cake, thick cream, and fresh fruit. Some trifles also contain a small amount of alcohol (such as Cointreau, rum, or kirsch).

Our book offers an informative approach to fruit desserts. Each chapter introduces you to a seasonal selection of fruit, and the recipes include headnotes to help you learn more about the dessert. We have also included kitchen hints to educate you about baking techniques that make baking easier. Near the end of the book you will find a pantry section with recipes we refer to throughout this book, as well as a page of resources.

Happy baking!

Julie's Philosophy and Baking Tips

I am not a fussy baker. I believe that simple movements and quality ingredients bring desserts to their highest potential. Full-flavored fruits in season need little coaxing from sugar and flavorings to find their place on your dessert table. Here are a few simple guidelines I use.

WEIGHTS AND MEASURES

For accuracy, it is important to use the correct vessel to measure ingredients. Or better yet, treat yourself to an electronic scale and weigh your ingredients for the best results. Over time, ingredients like flour, cocoa, and confectioners' sugar absorb moisture and get packed down, which means that measuring cups are a less-than-accurate tool for measuring these ingredients. Investing in a small digital scale that displays pounds and ounces will help you measure ingredients with the same accuracy as a professional. Here are measurement guidelines for specific ingredients.

Fruit: Because fruit comes in all different colors, shapes, and sizes, I rely on a weight measurement for prepped fruit when determining how much fruit should be used in a recipe. If the recipe calls for a certain weight or cup measurement of fruit, the recipe assumes you have already peeled, cored, trimmed, stemmed, hulled, or otherwise prepped the fruit before weighing or measuring it. Therefore, we suggest you buy a larger weight than the recipe indicates as you will lose some weight or volume in the process of prepping the fruit. The number of apples, pears, etc. is merely an estimate. Plus, you can always snack on any extra fruit as you prepare the dessert.

Dry ingredients: Measuring cups for dry ingredients come in metal or plastic (I prefer metal) and usually come in increments of $\frac{1}{4}$, $\frac{1}{3}$, $\frac{1}{2}$, and 1 cup. I use the fluff, scoop, and swoop method when I measure dry ingredients: slightly fluff up the ingredient (especially flour), scoop up the ingredient so that it overflows the cup, then use a straight edge, such as the back of a knife, to sweep off (or swoop) the excess. When measuring brown sugar, pack the sugar into the cup, then carefully sweep off any excess. Measuring cups with a pour spout are for measuring liquid ingredients and should never be used to measure dry ingredients.

Wet ingredients: Use a glass measuring cup on a flat surface.

OVEN TEMPERATURE

I used a conventional gas oven for all of the baked recipes in this book. I suggest buying an inexpensive oven thermometer to keep in your oven at all times because the oven thermostat is not always reliable. A convection oven would be fantastic for the buckles, shortbread cookies, and cakes. If you use one, reduce the oven temperature by 25 degrees and keep a close eye on your dessert, as convection ovens bake more quickly. For pies, cobblers, crisps, and pandowdies, it is best to use the conventional heating method and have the heat come from the bottom. You know your oven the best (where the hot spots are and where to put your baked goods to get the best color), so take our baking times as suggestions and focus on the recipe's telltale doneness cues as the accurate measure of when to take the dessert out of the oven.

Preheated baking stones are great for baking a pie, cobbler, tart, crisp, or galette because they retain their heat, allowing the dessert to bake from the bottom up. This process creates such wonders as a golden (not soggy) bottom crust. Stones need a head start, so preheat them at least 45 minutes before your dessert goes into the oven.

When baking a pie, cobbler, or crisp, just place your pan or dish directly on the stone. I like to make a foil tray with an edge, and then lay it beneath the pie to collect any juice that may bubble over; this is unnecessary for a cobbler or crisp. For a galette, I find it easiest to keep it on a baking sheet and place the sheet directly on the stone.

FREEZING

The freezer is the pastry baker's dear friend, as so many products can be made ahead of time then used for easy last-minute desserts. When well wrapped, many raw components such as pie pastry, short dough, crisp or crumble toppings, and shortbread cookie dough can be stored for up to 3 months without a problem. So feel free to double or triple the recipes and keep some extra available for the next dessert that you make. Be sure to carefully wrap, label, and date anything you tuck into the freezer. I also freeze my whole, unbaked pies, which I feel makes them even better! Popping a pie in the oven directly from the freezer means your butter and fruit will take longer to melt, which allows the pie crust to bake up before the filling and creates a lovely golden bottom crust and a flakier pastry. You will need to increase your baking time by 15 to 25 minutes for a frozen pie.

I also freeze already-baked products, including shortbread cookies (which even taste great frozen), chiffon cake, Bundt cakes, and buckles. Again, do not forget to carefully wrap, label, and date the baked products before freezing them. They will not keep as long as unbaked products, so only freeze them for a month at most.

BAKING DISH EQUIVALENTS

We suggest ideal size equipment and baking vessels in each recipe, but if you do not have the precise pan, use the nearest equivalent based on the type of dish. Just be aware that the baking time will need to be adjusted when using a different size pan.

9 by $1\frac{1}{4}$-inch pie pan = 4 cups or 1 quart

9 by $1\frac{1}{2}$-inch pie pan = 5 cups or $1\frac{1}{4}$ quarts

$9\frac{1}{2}$ by 2-inch deep-dish pie pan = 7 cups or $1\frac{3}{4}$ quarts

8 by 8 by 2-inch square pan = 8 cups or 2 quarts

9 by 9 by $1\frac{1}{2}$-inch square pan = 8 cups or 2 quarts

9 by 9 by 2-inch pan = 10 cups or $2\frac{1}{2}$ quarts

$6\frac{1}{2}$ by $3\frac{1}{2}$-inch small Bundt pan = $5\frac{1}{2}$ cups or $1\frac{1}{3}$ quarts

9 by 3-inch Bundt pan = 10 cups or $2\frac{1}{4}$ quarts

10 by $3\frac{1}{2}$-inch Bundt pan = 12 cups or 3 quarts

$8\frac{1}{2}$ by 11 by 2-inch rectangular baking dish = 8 cups or 2 quarts

9 by 13 by 2-inch rectangular baking dish = 12 cups or 3 quarts

$12\frac{1}{4}$ by $8\frac{3}{4}$ by $2\frac{1}{2}$-inch oval baking dish = 8 cups or 2 quarts

9 by 2-inch round cake pan = 8 cups or 2 quarts

$9\frac{1}{2}$ by $2\frac{1}{2}$-inch springform pan = 10 cups or $2\frac{1}{2}$ quarts

9 by 3-inch springform pan = 11 cups or $2\frac{3}{4}$ quarts

THE BAKER'S BATTERY

- High-quality stainless steel chef's knife
- High-quality stainless steel paring knife
- Digital scale
- Set of measuring spoons
- Set of dry measuring cups
- 1-cup liquid measuring cup
- 2-quart liquid measuring cup
- Wooden spoons
- Whisk
- Rubber spatula
- Plastic scrapers
- Bench scraper
- Sifter
- Fine-mesh sieve
- Half-size sheet pans or baking sheets
- Pie pans
- Tart pans, including one with a removable bottom
- Pie crust shield
- 9-inch square pan
- 9-inch round pan
- 9 by 13-inch baking pan
- Bundt pan
- 2-quart and 3-quart baking dishes
- 9-inch cast-iron skillet
- Custard cups (also called ramekins)
- Rolling pin
- Offset spatula
- Microplane for zesting citrus
- Parchment paper or Silpat baking mat
- Metal mixing bowls
- Pastry brush
- Good oven mitts
- Food mill
- Electric mixer (preferably a stand mixer)
- Food processor
- Spice grater

What is my favorite tool? Simply, my hands! What better tool does a baker need? They are always there, they need no special cleaning other than some hot water and soap, do not require electricity, and they are so versatile. They can cut, press, roll, knead, and shape . . . it is a little messy at first, but once you start using your hands, you will realize what fun it is! For many of the recipes, I recommend rubbing the dry ingredients together with your hands; this step ensures that any cornstarch is fully incorporated into the dry ingredients before any wet ingredients are added.

THE PASTRY KITCHEN'S CUPBOARD

What is my favorite ingredient? I have two: unsalted high-fat butter (also called "European-style" butter) and fine sea salt. While it may seem odd to insist on butter that is unsalted and then add salt anyway, it makes a difference because it allows me to carefully control the flavor of what I bake. I want to choose when I add salt and how much salt is part of my product . . . and none of my baked goods go without it! Even if it is just a pinch, tad, morsel, or whatever you want to call it, salt is the ingredient that brings it all together. And I choose sea salt over all of the other salts available because of its pure clean flavor; I also prefer fine (not coarse) sea salt because the crystals need to dissolve easily in baked goods.

- Unsalted butter
- Sugars: granulated, brown (I use light in most of my recipes unless I want a deeper molasses flavor, in which case I use dark), and confectioners'
- Flours: all-purpose flour, cake flour, and rice flour (Use the latter for rolling out pastry and making shortbread.)
- Vanilla extract and vanilla beans
- Fine sea salt (Taste it compared to other salts; it is just better.)
- Fresh spices (Buy small quantities in bulk from busy stores to help ensure that they are fresh.)

- Nuts (Store them in an airtight container in the freezer for freshness.)
- Fresh ripe produce (Your local farmers market is the best source.)
- Fresh dairy products and large eggs
- Leaveners (Buy baking soda and baking powder annually if not more often; they lose their strength when they get old.)
- Cocoa: Dutch-processed and natural
- Grains: oats, cornmeal, and so on

I believe in the integrity of each ingredient. Do not be afraid to taste them individually: pure vanilla, granulated cane sugar, unbleached flours, unsalted "European-style" butter, sea salt, and fruits. At the peak of their flavor, these are the components that will bring your desserts to life.

spring ⟞⟝⟞⟝⟞⟝⟞⟝⟞⟝

The beginning of spring holds such promise: bulbs pop out of the ground, birds begin to sing, the skies seem brighter and bluer. But alas, spring is still a time of want for the home cook who treasures fresh fruit. We look outside, check our gardens, and walk past the stalls of the farmers markets, eagerly awaiting the flush of fruit that beckons throughout summer and fall. Early spring, unfortunately, holds no such bounty—except, of course, for rhubarb, which placates the impatient among us!

Rhubarb requires a cold winter and cool weather during its growing season, so while you will find it plentiful in the Pacific Northwest, you probably will not find it at farmers markets in the southern United States. It appears in our markets in April, at which time customers often lunge toward this vibrant, hot pink plant and wave it in the air as evidence that winter is over and spring really is here. (Note that rhubarb is actually a vegetable, but since "rustic vegetable desserts" does not sound catchy enough for a cookbook sequel, we have slipped it in here instead.)

Rhubarb stalks are commonly red, although green varieties, often kissed with pink speckles, also exist. Crimson is a popular variety of rhubarb in the Pacific Northwest. Its red color permeates the hearty stalk and makes a bright impact on the plate. Tart and acidic, rhubarb makes an impact on the palate, too. While many people believe that rhubarb and strawberries are the perfect marriage (such as in the Rhubarb Cream Cheese Pie with Fresh Strawberries, page 26), there are others who think adding fruit to a rhubarb pie is sacrilegious. I am in the camp that enjoys coupling rhubarb with different fruits. Rhubarb's tartness mellows when blended with apples in a pandowdy (page 16), and becomes enhanced when coupled with cherries in a brown betty (page 22). If you are a raving fan of tanginess, go all out for the Lemon Buttermilk Rhubarb Bundt Cake (page 36). You will not be disappointed.

By late spring, various fruits join rhubarb at the produce stand. Cherries, in both sweet and sour varieties, appear in May and June. Over the next month or two, different varieties ripen at various times, so you can enjoy a staggered appreciation for the fruit. Sweet cherry varieties include early ripening Chelans, inky dark Lamberts, golden blushing Rainiers, mahogany red Bings, and late-season Vans. Sour cherries include English, Morello, and Montmorency varieties. If you have never baked with sour cherries, now is the time to branch out. They are a prized fruit for mouthwatering pies and cobblers, as anyone who has tasted sour cherries will tell you.

I joke with visitors to Portland in June that summer does not begin until July 5—and the joke's not funny because it is true. In Oregon, the cool weather and spring rains continue through June. Luckily for us, June is the month when, long anticipated by all, strawberries begin to arrive at the market. Varieties such as Totem, Hood, and Seascape dominate Oregon's farmers markets, but adventurous farmers offer other, lesser-known varieties, like candy-sweet alpine strawberries. By the time strawberries arrive, we breathe a sigh of relief, knowing it will not be long until it feels like summer and the markets burst with more fruit. In the meantime, however, we are more than satisfied with the sweet taste of a strawberry as we make our way home from the market with the basket within arm's reach.

As we begin to enjoy a new cycle of fresh-grown fruit, spring's bounty beckons us into the kitchen. Here are some tips for choosing fruit at the market in spring.

CHERRIES

Cherries should be taut, plump, and bright. Wrinkles mean they are past their peak. Look at the stems to see if the cherries were picked recently, in which case the stems will be green; brown or black brittle stems indicate that they are older. Cherries do not ripen once they are picked, so taste one for sweetness (or tartness, depending on which flavor you're seeking!). After purchase, immediately store cherries in the refrigerator, where they will stay fresh for several days. Avoid placing cherries in the sun or anywhere warm, as they will soften quickly.

RHUBARB

The color of rhubarb stalks (or, more technically, petioles) varies from deep red to speckled pink to light green depending on the variety and is not an indication of ripeness or flavor. In Oregon, Crimson Red is popular for baking. In other parts of the country, look for Victoria (a green stalk with pink speckles) or Valentine (deep red, of course). Look for stalks that are turgid and have glossy skin. Limp, flexible rhubarb is a sign that it was picked a while ago and will not taste as juicy and bright. Avoid stalks that are either too thin (and thus less flavorful) or too thick (possibly too fibrous). The leaves of the rhubarb plant are poisonous if eaten, so they are usually removed before the stalks get to the market. If any leaf part remains, note whether it is green and fresh or brown and old. When buying rhubarb, remember to buy extra if the rhubarb has leafy green tops or butt ends that came straight out of the ground because you will be trimming this all away to prep your rhubarb for our recipes.

STRAWBERRIES

Strawberries should be plump and well rounded. They should have a natural shine and a rich red color free of white, green, or hard seedy tips. When purchasing a basket of strawberries, check that unripe or overripe berries are not buried beneath a ripe layer on top. Strawberries do not sweeten after they are picked, so if you can, taste one for ripeness. Their caps should appear bright green. Do not purchase strawberries without caps, as they may be overripe and not of good quality. To ensure the best flavor, use strawberries as soon as possible after picking or purchasing them. They are highly perishable, so store them in the refrigerator if you will not be using them immediately.

apple and rhubarb pandowdy

This pandowdy brings together the last apples of winter and the first spring rhubarb, bridging the seasons in a dessert. The smooth, balanced taste of apples cuts the tart, sassy bite of rhubarb, which might otherwise scare away someone unfamiliar with rhubarb from tucking into this delicious pandowdy.

BAKING TIME: 45 TO 50 MINUTES / SERVES 8 TO 10

1 tablespoon unsalted butter, at room temperature, for pan

¼ recipe (1 disk) All-Butter Pie Pastry (page 151)

3 to 4 tart apples, peeled, cored, quartered, and sliced ½ inch thick (1 pound prepped)

1¾ pounds rhubarb, trimmed and sliced ½ inch thick (5 cups or 1¼ pounds prepped)

Zest and juice of 1 large lemon (page 134)

¾ cup packed (5¾ ounces) brown sugar

2½ tablespoons cornstarch

1 teaspoon ground cinnamon

¼ teaspoon fine sea salt

Vanilla Bean Ice Cream (page 146), for serving (optional)

Preheat the oven to 425°F. Butter a 9-inch deep-dish pie pan or cast-iron skillet or a 9-inch square baking pan.

Toss the apples, rhubarb, lemon zest, and lemon juice together in a large bowl. Separately, rub together the brown sugar, cornstarch, cinnamon, and salt, then add to the fruit mixture and stir to combine. Transfer the mixture to the prepared pan.

Roll out the pie pastry to roughly the size of the pan. Top the apples and rhubarb with the pastry, tucking in any excess pastry between the fruit and the side of the pan. This is a rustic dessert, so there is no need to spend any extra time making it look fancy; the beauty lies in its rough look. Cut a few steam vents in the crust, then place the pandowdy on a baking sheet to collect any drips. Bake for 20 minutes, then turn the oven down to 350°F and bake for an additional 25 to 30 minutes, or until the crust is golden and the fruit is bubbling around the edges or through the steam vents.

Cool the pandowdy for 1 hour before serving, topped with a scoop of Vanilla Bean Ice Cream.

Storage: Covered with a tea towel, the pandowdy will keep at room temperature for up to 3 days.

rhubarb fool

The fool originated in England in the fifteenth or sixteenth century. It is a simple dessert that combines tart fruit with whipped cream. The British traditionally made this dessert with gooseberries, but in spring rhubarb is the perfect choice, with its bright, tart flavor. A very simple dessert to prepare (we wince to say any fool can make it), this recipe calls for cooking a compote and then folding in whipped cream. It is elegant served with a shortbread cookie, which adds a delicious crispy element. To really doll it up, add a Candied Rhubarb Strip.

 **SERVES 6**

1½ pounds rhubarb, trimmed and sliced ½ inch thick (about 4 cups or 1 pound prepped)

½ cup honey

Zest and juice of 1 orange

2 tablespoons finely chopped candied ginger

½ vanilla bean, split

Pinch of fine sea salt

¾ cup heavy cream

1 tablespoon granulated sugar

CANDIED RHUBARB STRIPS

1 stalk rhubarb

½ cup (3½ ounces) granulated sugar

½ cup water

SEE HINT:
"WHIPPING
CREAM"
PAGE 145

To make the fool, put the rhubarb, honey, orange zest and juice, candied ginger, vanilla bean, and salt in a saucepan over medium heat. Stir to combine, then cover and cook, stirring every few minutes, for 10 minutes, until the mixture has come to a boil and the rhubarb has softened. Remove from the heat and allow to cool, then remove the vanilla bean. Transfer the compote to a bowl, and refrigerate, uncovered, for at least 30 minutes, until very cold.

Whip the cream and sugar until soft peaks form, either by hand or using an electric mixer on medium speed (see Whipping Cream, page 145). Set aside ⅓ cup of the compote to garnish the dessert, then fold the remaining compote into the whipped cream. Spoon the fool into six ½-cup glasses or dishes and chill for 1 hour before serving topped with the remaining compote.

Storage: This fool is best served the day it is made, but any leftovers can be covered with plastic wrap and stored in the refrigerator for up to 2 days.

If you would like to garnish the dessert with candied rhubarb strips, make them first: Preheat the oven to 200°F. Line a baking sheet with a Silpat mat or lightly greased parchment paper.

CONTINUED

rhubarb fool, continued

Cut the rhubarb into 6-inch lengths, then cut each piece into strips $1/4$ inch to $1/8$ inch thick with a good peeler, a mandoline, or a well-positioned knife. Combine the sugar and water in a saucepan over high heat and bring to a boil. Cook and stir until the sugar is dissolved, then remove from the heat. Dip the rhubarb ribbons into the syrup, then place them on the prepared baking sheet, laying them out flat and ensuring that they do not touch each other.

Bake for about 45 minutes, until dry. While they are still warm, twist the strips into shapes, wrapping them around your finger or the handle of a clean wooden spoon. Use immediately, or store in an airtight container for up to 3 days.

KITCHEN HINT:

Vanilla Beans

When buying vanilla beans, look for plump, moist, shiny pods and avoid any that are dried up and brittle. Store vanilla pods wrapped in plastic, away from light, and never in the refrigerator, which dries them out. To use the seeds inside the pod, lay the vanilla pod flat on a cutting board and slice it open lengthwise with a small, sharp knife. Using the tip of your knife, you can then scrape out the seeds. Once the seeds have been scraped out, the pod is still filled with flavor and can be used to infuse a mug of hot milk or a pitcher of lemonade. Rinse and dry the pod between uses and store as usual. Once most of the flavor is gone, tuck the pod into your sugar jar to add a subtle flavor and aroma.

rhubarb compote two ways

Rhubarb is a tart plant; it is actually a vegetable, not a fruit. It is commonly stewed, sweetened, and baked in a pie—so often, in fact, that it has acquired the slang name "pie plant." Here we use it in two versions of compote which is by definition a cooked fruit. The first recipe is classic cooked rhubarb compote. In the second recipe, we propose a raw alternative to the stewed, jammy version that usually graces one's bowl in spring. Raw rhubarb is slightly crunchy and has a bright and delightful flavor when macerated (that term simply means allowing it to soften in its own juice). If you really want to experiment, consider adding fresh rosemary or lavender to the bowl of raw rhubarb to infuse an herbal flavor.

 **SERVES 6**

THE FIRST WAY: STEWED

2¼ pounds rhubarb (6 cups or about 1½ pounds prepped)

1 cup freshly squeezed orange juice (about 2 large oranges)

½ cup (3½ ounces) granulated sugar

¼ teaspoon ground cardamom

Trim away the leaves and butt ends of the rhubarb, as well as any stringy or damaged parts (a peeler is handy for this task). Cut each stalk in half lengthwise, then chop into 1-inch pieces. Strain the orange juice into a large, heavy, nonreactive pot over medium-high heat and cook, stirring occasionally, until the juice is reduced by half. Add the sugar and cardamom and stir until dissolved, then add the rhubarb, cover, and simmer for about 10 minutes, until the rhubarb is soft and broken down. Serve warm or chilled.

Storage: Stored in an airtight container in the refrigerator, the compote will keep for up to 3 days.

THE SECOND WAY: RAW

2¼ pounds rhubarb (6 cups or about 1½ pounds prepped)

½ cup (3½ ounces) granulated sugar

¼ cup freshly squeezed orange juice (about ½ orange)

Trim away the leaves and butt ends of the rhubarb, as well as any stringy or damaged parts (a peeler is handy for this task). Cut the rhubarb lengthwise into ¼-inch strips, then cut crosswise into ¼-inch pieces. Put the rhubarb in a bowl, add the sugar and juice, and toss until evenly combined. Cover and let sit at room temperature for at least 6 hours, and preferably overnight.

Storage: Stored in an airtight container in the refrigerator, the compote will keep for up to 3 days.

rhubarb and bing cherry brown betty

This recipe bridges two seasons, combining the end of rhubarb with the beginning of cherries. Any sweet cherries will work; we have made this betty with Royal Ann, Bing, Lambert, and Rainier cherries. This recipe is a different spin on a betty. Instead of bread crumbs, it calls for shortbread cookie crumbs. For ease or speed of preparation, you can use store-bought shortbread (such as Lorna Doone Shortbread Cookies) in lieu of homemade.

+⟫═ BAKING TIME: 45 MINUTES / SERVES 8 TO 12 ═⟪+

2 tablespoons unsalted butter, at room temperature, for pan

1 pound Vanilla Bean Shortbread (page 155), crushed (approximately 18 cookies, or 4 cups crushed)

1 cup (7 ounces) granulated sugar

1 teaspoon ground cinnamon

2¼ pounds rhubarb, trimmed and sliced ½ inch thick (about 6 cups or 1½ pounds prepped)

2 cups (12 ounces) Bing cherries, fresh or frozen, pitted

2 tablespoons kirsch or brandy

Chantilly cream (page 145), for serving148

Preheat the oven to 400°F. Generously butter a 3-quart baking dish.

Rub the sugar and cinnamon together in a large bowl, then add the rhubarb and cherries and toss to combine. Stir in the liquor, then let sit for 15 minutes to draw some of the juices from the rhubarb and cherries.

Evenly spread half of the crushed cookies in the prepared pan, then add the rhubarb mixture and all of its juices and gently spread it over the crumbs. Top with the remaining crushed cookies.

Cover with aluminum foil and bake in the middle of the oven for 30 minutes. Remove the foil and, using the back of a large offset spatula or something similar to it, gently press down on the betty to ensure the rhubarb mixture is submerged in its juices. Bake uncovered for an additional 15 minutes, or until the top is lightly browned. Test the rhubarb with a paring knife to ensure that it is soft. Cool for 20 minutes before serving, topped with a dollop of Chantilly cream.

Storage: This betty is best served the day it is made, but any leftovers can be wrapped in plastic wrap and kept at room temperature for 2 to 3 days.

sour cherry cobbler

Sour cherries, also called tart cherries or pie cherries, are seldom found in grocery stores and appear only fleetingly at farmers markets because of their short season. They are grown in the Pacific Northwest and the Midwest, where they are harvested in late June or early July. The most popular sour cherry is the Montmorency, a glassy red cherry with translucent golden juice. Morellos, another variety of sour cherry, are darker in color and give off an inky purple juice. Both are excellent for baking. You can freeze fresh sour cherries by pitting them and popping them into a plastic bag, but do not delay in doing so, since sour cherries do not last long once they are picked!

BAKING TIME: 50 TO 55 MINUTES / SERVES 8 TO 12

1 tablespoon unsalted butter, at room temperature, for pan

FRUIT FILLING

¾ cup (5¼ ounces) granulated sugar

3 tablespoons cornstarch

¼ teaspoon fine sea salt

4 cups (1½ pounds) sour cherries, fresh or frozen, pitted

2 tablespoons pure vanilla extract or cherry liqueur

Preheat the oven to 375°F. Butter a 3-quart baking dish.

To make the fruit filling, rub the sugar, cornstarch, and salt together in a bowl. Add the cherries, toss until evenly coated, then gently stir in the vanilla. Spoon the fruit into the prepared pan, being sure to scrape the bowl well.

CONTINUED

sour cherry cobbler, continued

BISCUIT

1¼ cups (6¼ ounces) all-purpose flour

¾ cup unsifted (4 ounces) cake flour

1 tablespoon granulated sugar, plus 1 tablespoon to top biscuits

1 teaspoon baking powder

½ teaspoon fine sea salt

½ cup (4 ounces) cold unsalted butter, cut into small cubes

¾ cup plus 1 tablespoon cold buttermilk

¼ cup heavy cream

To make the biscuit, whisk the flours, 1 tablespoon of the sugar, the baking powder, and salt together in a bowl. Add the butter and toss until evenly coated. Using your fingertips or a pastry blender, cut in the butter until the size of large peas. (Alternatively, you can put the dry ingredients in a food processor and pulse to combine. Add the butter and pulse until the butter is the size of large peas, then transfer to a bowl.) Combine ¾ cup of the buttermilk and the cream, then pour into the dry ingredients and stir just until the dry ingredients are moistened. The dough will be crumbly, with large pieces of butter still visible.

Turn the dough out onto a lightly floured work surface and gently press the dough together to form a rectangle, then roll out to a thickness of ⅓ inch. Cut out twelve 2½-inch round or square biscuits, rerolling the scraps as needed. Place the biscuits atop the fruit filling, then brush the tops of the biscuits with the 1 tablespoon buttermilk and sprinkle with the remaining 1 tablespoon sugar.

Bake for about 50 minutes, or until the biscuits are golden and the filling is bubbling all over. Serve warm.

Storage: Covered with a tea towel, the cobbler can be stored at room temperature for up to 2 days. Reheat in a 300°F oven until warmed through.

rhubarb cream cheese pie
with fresh strawberries

This recipe comes from my best friend, Stacy Carter, whose mom was always baking something for us to enjoy. This tiered dessert is no exception: rhubarb hides beneath a sweet cream cheese custard, while fresh strawberries sit on top to tempt anyone passing through the kitchen. The tastes alternate in your mouth from tart to creamy, creamy to sweet. One word of caution: be sure not to overbake the pie, as it could crack. —*Julie*

✄ BAKING TIME: 40 TO 45 MINUTES / SERVES 8 TO 12 ✄

¼ recipe (1 disk) All-Butter Pie Pastry (page 151), prebaked in a 9-inch pie pan and cooled

½ cup (3½ ounces) granulated sugar

1 tablespoon cornstarch

1½ pounds rhubarb, trimmed and thinly sliced (about 4 cups or 1 pound prepped)

CUSTARD

1½ cups (12 ounces) cream cheese, at room temperature

½ cup (3½ ounces) granulated sugar

2 eggs

1 teaspoon pure vanilla extract

⅛ teaspoon fine sea salt

2 cups strawberries, hulled and halved

2 tablespoons confectioners' sugar

Preheat the oven to 425°F.

Rub the sugar and cornstarch together in a large bowl, then add the rhubarb and toss until evenly coated. Spoon the rhubarb mixture into the prebaked pie crust. Bake in the middle of the oven for 15 minutes, then remove the pie from the oven and turn the oven down to 350°F.

Meanwhile, make the custard. Using a handheld mixer with beaters or a stand mixer with the paddle attachment, beat the cream cheese and sugar on medium speed until light and fluffy. Add the eggs one at a time, beating until smooth after each addition and scraping down the sides of the bowl occasionally. Stir in the vanilla and salt.

Pour the custard into the pie and spread it evenly and smoothly over the rhubarb. Return the pie to the oven (now at 350°F) and bake for 25 to 30 minutes, or until the custard puffs up around the edges but is still slightly wobbly in the middle. (Do not worry; as the pie cools, the center will firm up.) Cool to room temperature on a wire rack.

Place the strawberries atop the pie and dust with confectioners' sugar just before serving (a sieve works well for this), or serve the berries alongside individual slices of pie.

Storage: The pie can be made a day in advance, in which case you should refrigerate it and top with the strawberries just before serving. Covered with plastic wrap, any leftovers will keep in the refrigerator for 2 to 3 days.

rhubarb buckle with ginger crumb

This buckle thumbs its nose at winter with both its color and its flavor. The cake is dotted with hot pink slices of rhubarb, and between ginger's spicy heat and rhubarb's tart tang, you will never feel the chill in the air. Buckles make an elegant breakfast.

+≈ BAKING TIME: 45 TO 50 MINUTES / SERVES 8 TO 12 ≈+

1 tablespoon unsalted butter, at room temperature, for pan

GINGER CRUMB TOPPING

⅓ cup (2¼ ounces) granulated sugar

¼ cup (1¼ ounces) all-purpose flour

¼ cup (1 ounce) finely chopped candied ginger

2 tablespoons unsalted butter, melted

CAKE

1¾ cups (8¾ ounces) all-purpose flour

1 teaspoon baking powder

1 teaspoon dried ginger

½ teaspoon baking soda

½ teaspoon fine sea salt

¾ cup (6 ounces) unsalted butter, at room temperature

1 cup (7 ounces) granulated sugar

2 eggs

¾ cup buttermilk, at room temperature

1 pound rhubarb, trimmed and thinly sliced (about 2½ cups or 10 ounces prepped)

Preheat the oven to 350°F. Butter a 9-inch round baking pan.

To make the ginger crumb topping, mix the sugar, flour, and candied ginger together in a bowl, then stir in the melted butter. Put the crumb in the freezer while you mix the cake batter. (This chills the crumb so it will not immediately melt into the cake when baked.)

To make the cake, whisk the flour, baking powder, ginger, baking soda, and salt together in a bowl. Using a handheld mixer with beaters or a stand mixer with the paddle attachment, cream the butter and sugar together on medium-high speed until light and fluffy, 3 to 5 minutes. Add the eggs one at a time, scraping down the sides of the bowl after each addition. Stir in the flour mixture in three additions alternating with the buttermilk in two additions, beginning and ending with the dry ingredients and scraping down the sides of the bowl occasionally. Gently fold in the rhubarb.

Spread the batter into the prepared pan, then sprinkle the ginger crumb over the cake. Bake for 45 to 50 minutes, or until lightly golden and firm on top.

Storage: Wrapped in plastic wrap, the cake will keep at room temperature for 2 to 3 days.

fresh strawberry and ricotta tart

I always think of an Italian grandmother when I make this ricotta tart—you know, the one who would bring you a perfectly scooped ice cream cone when you were at a sleep-over, having just whipped up the ice cream and probably the cone as well. They were the ones who never had a recipe for anything; they just knew that a little bit of this and a little bit of that made something incredibly yummy. As I am not Italian, I have taken the liberty of replacing some of the traditional ricotta with cream cheese for a smoother texture. Small strawberries are best for this tart, but you can also use large strawberries if you slice them in half. —*Julie*

BAKING TIME: 30 MINUTES / SERVES 8 TO 12

1 recipe Short Dough (page 152), baked in a 10-inch fluted tart pan with a removable bottom, cooled

1 cup (8 ounces) whole-milk ricotta

⅔ cup (6 ounces) cream cheese, at room temperature

¾ cup (5¼ ounces) granulated sugar

Seeds scraped from ½ vanilla bean (see Vanilla Beans, page 20)

½ teaspoon fine sea salt

¼ teaspoon freshly grated nutmeg

2 eggs

1 tablespoon pure vanilla extract

3 dry pints (6 cups) strawberries, hulled, and halved if large

½ cup strawberry jam

Preheat the oven to 350°F.

Using a handheld mixer with beaters or a stand mixer with the paddle attachment, mix the ricotta, cream cheese, sugar, vanilla bean seeds, salt, and nutmeg on medium speed. Add the eggs one at a time, beating until smooth after each addition and scraping down the sides of the bowl occasionally. Stir in the vanilla.

Pour the filling into the prebaked tart shell and bake in the middle of the oven for 30 minutes, or until the edges have puffed up but the middle is still quite wobbly. (Do not worry; as the tart cools, the center will firm up.) Cool to room temperature on a wire rack, then chill in the refrigerator for 1 hour.

Just before serving, put the strawberries in a bowl. Warm the strawberry jam in small saucepan over low heat, then strain the jam over the strawberries and toss to coat. Arrange the berries on top of the tart and serve immediately. Alternatively, you could omit the jam and serve the berries alongside the tart.

Storage: The tart can be made a day in advance, in which case you should refrigerate it and top with the strawberries just before serving. Covered with plastic wrap, any leftovers will keep in the refrigerator for 2 to 3 days.

rhubarb, oat, and pecan crumble

When Baker & Spice started out as a booth at the Portland Farmers Market, the rhubarb items on display were usually passed over for pastries made with more familiar fruit. Today, it seems we are in the midst of a rhubarb renaissance, as the bakery cannot make enough rhubarb pastries to meet the demand! Rhubarb's tart, sassy flavor, once so foreign to the mainstream, now has a devout following. For this dessert, the rhubarb filling is unadulterated by other flavors, while pecan and oats add depth to the crumble topping.

❈ BAKING TIME: 45 TO 50 MINUTES / SERVES 8 TO 12 ❈

1 tablespoon unsalted butter, at room temperature, for dish

CRUMBLE

¾ cup (3¾ ounces) all-purpose flour

½ cup (2 ounces) rolled oats

½ cup packed (3¾ ounces) brown sugar

½ cup (2⅛ ounces) chopped pecans

½ teaspoon fine sea salt

¼ cup (2 ounces) unsalted butter, melted

RHUBARB FILLING

1 cup (7 ounces) granulated sugar

2 tablespoons cornstarch

3½ pounds rhubarb, trimmed and chopped into 1-inch pieces (about 10½ cups or 2 pounds, 6 ounces prepped)

1 tablespoon pure vanilla extract

Preheat the oven to 375°F. Butter a 3-quart baking dish.

To make the crumble, mix the flour, oats, brown sugar, pecans, and salt together in a bowl. Stir in the butter, then press the mixture together with your hands to form a few small clumps. Put the topping in the freezer while you assemble the filling.

To make the rhubarb filling, rub the granulated sugar and cornstarch together in a bowl, then add the rhubarb and vanilla and toss until evenly coated.

Transfer the rhubarb mixture into the prepared pan and scatter the crumble topping over the top. Bake for about 45 minutes, or until the topping is golden and the filling bubbles up through the topping. Cool for 20 minutes before serving.

Storage: This crisp is best served the day it is made, but any leftovers can be wrapped in plastic wrap and eaten for breakfast the next morning or kept at room temperature for 2 to 3 days.

boozy dried cherry, chocolate, and hazelnut bread pudding

While we have tucked this recipe into the spring chapter because of the cherries, you could make it any time of year since it uses dried fruit. The dried sour cherries can be soaked in liquor or apple cider, depending on your preference. Since the cherries need to soak for at least 1 hour, plan ahead when making this dessert. Use a simple bread for this recipe, as the strong flavor of the cherries and chocolate are likely to overwhelm any flavors in the bread. This decadent bread pudding is even more sinfully delicious if served with the Vanilla Sauce (page 149) spiked with cherry liqueur. Enjoy!

BAKING TIME: 50 TO 60 MINUTES / SERVES 8 TO 12

1 tablespoon unsalted butter, at room temperature, for dish

1 cup (6 ounces) dried sour cherries

½ cup brandy

1 cup heavy cream

1¼ cups (8 ounces) bittersweet chocolate chips

3 cups whole milk

6 eggs

½ cup (3½ ounces) granulated sugar

2 teaspoons pure vanilla extract

½ teaspoon fine sea salt

1 pound stale bread, cut into 1-inch cubes (8 to 9 cups)

1 cup (4 ounces) chopped toasted hazelnuts (see Kitchen Hint, page 101)

2 tablespoons confectioners' sugar

Vanilla Sauce (page 149), for serving (optional)

Soak the dried cherries in the brandy for at least 1 hour.

Heat the cream until barely boiling, then immediately remove from the heat. Add the chocolate, cover, and let sit for 5 minutes, then gently stir until the chocolate is melted and uniformly incorporated. Whisk in 1 cup of the milk. Separately, whisk the eggs, sugar, vanilla, and salt together in a bowl large enough to hold all of the pudding ingredients. Whisk in the remaining 2 cups milk, then the chocolate mixture. Stir in the bread cubes and the cherries and brandy. Chill the mixture in the refrigerator for 1 hour, stirring every 15 to 20 minutes so the custard absorbs evenly.

Preheat the oven to 325°F. Butter a 2-quart baking dish.

Pour the chilled mixture into the prepared pan and sprinkle with the hazelnuts, stirring slightly to work them into the top layer. Bake for 50 to 60 minutes, until the pudding has puffed up around the edges and the center is no longer runny. Cool for 20 minutes before sifting the confectioners' sugar over the top. Serve with the cherry-spiked Vanilla Sauce alongside.

Storage: This bread pudding is best served the day it is made, but any leftovers can be wrapped in plastic wrap and refrigerated for 2 to 3 days. Rewarm in a 300°F oven for 10 to 15 minutes.

upside-down sweet cherry cake

This recipe is trickier than others in this book in two respects: the caramel topping and the inversion of the cake both require attention. The trick to making the caramel is to stay at your stovetop; do not walk away at any point during the caramelizing process. Also, remember that the melted sugar will be extremely hot once you pour it in the pan, and the intense heat will persist long after your mind has moved on to making the rest of the recipe, so be careful. After the cake has baked and cooled and it is time to invert the cake onto a plate, be sure the plate is large and flat enough that you can easily flip the cake over. If you do this in one swift, confident motion, you will have no trouble. This wonderful cake is especially delicious served with a dollop of Chantilly cream (page 145).

━━ BAKING TIME: 60 TO 65 MINUTES / SERVES 10 TO 12 ━━

1 tablespoon unsalted butter, at room temperature, for pan

CARAMEL TOPPING

¼ cup (2 ounces) unsalted butter

¾ cup (5¼ ounces) granulated sugar

2 tablespoons freshly squeezed lemon juice (about ½ lemon)

4 cups (1½ pounds) pitted sweet cherries

Preheat the oven to 350°F. Butter a 9-inch square baking pan, preferably one with a nonstick surface.

To make the caramel topping, melt the butter in a sauté pan over medium heat, then stir in the granulated sugar and lemon juice with a wooden spoon. Turn the heat up to medium-high and bring the mixture to a boil. As it boils, it will become foamy and change color from beige to amber brown. Once it turns amber, remove it from the heat and pour the caramel into the prepared pan. Set aside to cool for about 10 minutes.

Place the cherries in a single layer on top of the caramel with the pitted sides facing up.

CONTINUED

SEE HINT: "MAKING CARAMEL" PAGE 71

upside-down sweet cherry cake, continued

CAKE

1¾ cups (8¾ ounces) all-purpose flour

1 teaspoon ground cinnamon

1 teaspoon baking powder

½ teaspoon baking soda

½ teaspoon fine sea salt

¾ cup (6 ounces) unsalted butter

1 cup plus 2 tablespoons (8 ounces) granulated sugar

Zest and juice of 1 orange

2 eggs, separated (see Kitchen Hint, page 157)

1 teaspoon pure vanilla extract

¾ cup (7½ ounces) sour cream

SEE HINT: "ZESTING CITRUS" PAGE 134

To make the cake, sift the flour, cinnamon, baking powder, baking soda, and salt together in a bowl. Using a hand-held mixer with beaters or a stand mixer with the paddle attachment, cream the butter, sugar, and orange zest together on medium-high speed for 3 to 5 minutes, until light and fluffy. Add the eggs yolks one at a time, scraping down the sides of the bowl after each addition, then stir in the orange juice and the vanilla. Stir in the flour mixture in three additions alternating with the sour cream in two additions, beginning and ending with the flour mixture and scraping down the sides of the bowl occasionally. The batter will be thick. In a clean bowl, whisk the egg whites until soft peaks form. Fold half of the whites into the batter, incorporating them fully before adding the second half.

Carefully pour the batter into the pan and gently spread in an even layer over the cherries.

Bake for 60 to 65 minutes, or until the top of the cake is firm and the center springs back when lightly touched. The cake will be very brown and might crack slightly in the middle; do not worry about any of this, as the cake just has a lot of moisture inside from the cherries, and it will be inverted before serving. Cool the cake in its pan on a wire rack for 45 minutes.

To flip the cake out of its pan, first run a knife around the edges, then place a flat plate or serving platter facedown over the top of the cake and quickly invert the cake onto the platter in one fell swoop.

Storage: Wrapped in plastic wrap, the cake will keep at room temperature for up to 3 days.

lemon buttermilk rhubarb bundt cake

Lemon Bundt cake is a spring and summer staple at Baker & Spice. Depending on what produce is in season, you might find the cake studded with rhubarb, blueberries, or cranberries. The result is a moist, yummy cake that gives new meaning to the term *comfort food*. The lemon glaze that coats the cake's exterior is quick to make and packs quite a zing. But do not worry; the cake has a mellow sweetness to balance the tangy glaze.

⊷ BAKING TIME: 60 TO 65 MINUTES / SERVES 10 TO 12 ⊶

1 tablespoon unsalted butter, at room temperature, for pan

CAKE

2½ cups plus 2 tablespoons (12½ ounces plus ⅝ ounce) all-purpose flour

2 teaspoons baking powder

1 teaspoon fine sea salt

1 cup (8 ounces) unsalted butter

1¾ cups (12 ounces) granulated sugar

Zest of 1 lemon

3 eggs

½ teaspoon lemon oil

¾ cup buttermilk

1 pound rhubarb, trimmed and very thinly sliced (3 cups or 12 ounces prepped)

LEMON GLAZE

2 cups (8½ ounces) sifted confectioners' sugar, or more as needed

Juice of 1 lemon juice

1 tablespoon soft unsalted butter

Preheat the oven to 350°F. Butter a 10-cup Bundt pan.

To make the cake, sift the 2½ cups flour, the baking powder, and salt together in a bowl. Using a handheld mixer with beaters or a stand mixer with the paddle attachment, cream the butter, sugar, and lemon zest together on medium-high speed for 3 to 5 minutes, until light and fluffy. Add the eggs one at a time, scraping down the sides of the bowl after each addition, then stir in the lemon oil. Stir in the flour mixture in three additions alternating with the buttermilk in two additions, beginning and ending with the flour mixture and scraping down the sides of the bowl occasionally. The batter will be very thick.

Toss the rhubarb with the 2 tablespoons flour and fold half of the rhubarb into the batter. Pour the batter into the prepared pan and sprinkle the remaining rhubarb on top.

Bake for 30 minutes, then rotate the pan and cook for an additional 30 minutes, or until the top of the cake is firm and the center springs back when lightly touched. Cool the cake in its pan on a wire rack for 30 minutes before inverting and removing the pan.

To make the lemon glaze, whisk the confectioners' sugar, lemon juice, and butter together. The mixture should be thick. If it is not, whisk in another tablespoon or two of confectioners' sugar. Spread the glaze over the cake as soon as you remove the cake from the pan.

Storage: Covered with a cake cover or plastic wrap, the cake will keep at room temperature for 3 to 4 days.

cherry almond bars

Who needs lemon bars when you have cherries? If you need to whip something up for a picnic and you have some cherries in your freezer, you can make this treat in no time.

1 tablespoon unsalted butter, at room temperature, for pan

FRUIT FILLING

3 cups (18 ounces) cherries, pitted and halved if small or quartered if large

½ cup (3½ ounces) granulated sugar

1 tablespoon cornstarch

¼ teaspoon fine sea salt

Zest and juice of 1 lemon

CRUST AND TOPPING

2¼ cups (11¼ ounces) all-purpose flour

½ cup packed (3¾ ounces) brown sugar

1 cup (4 ounces) sliced almonds

½ teaspoon fine sea salt

¾ cup (6 ounces) cold unsalted butter, cut into small cubes

1 egg

1 teaspoon pure vanilla extract

Preheat the oven to 350°F. Butter a 9-inch square baking pan.

To make the fruit filling, combine the cherries, sugar, cornstarch, salt, lemon zest, and lemon juice in a saucepan over medium-high heat. Bring to a boil, stirring occasionally, and boil for 1 minute to thicken.

To make the crust and topping, combine the flour, brown sugar, almonds, and salt in the bowl of a food processor. Add the butter and process until crumbly. Add the egg and vanilla and pulse just until the mixture comes together.

Press two-thirds of the mixture into the bottom of the prepared pan, then pour in the cherry filling. Press clumps of the remaining crumb mixture over the cherry filling.

Bake in the middle of the oven for 30 to 35 minutes, or until light golden brown and bubbling around the edge. Cool for 1 hour before cutting into bars.

Storage: Stored in an airtight container at room temperature, the bars will keep for up to 4 days.

SEE HINT: "ZESTING CITRUS" PAGE 134

strawberry shortcake

While strawberries are the classic fruit for shortcake, I've made this shortcake at various times using raspberries, blueberries, peaches, and Marionberries—any juicy fruit at the peak of its season tastes delicious with shortcake and Chantilly cream. Shortcakes are quick and easy to make, and they always get rave reviews. My teenage son, Graham, once made over twelve dozen of them for a family wedding party. To our surprise, there were none leftover at the end of the night! This recipe calls for a surprising amount of orange and lemon zest. Do not skimp on the zest; the citrus gives the biscuits a fresh, bright flavor that complements any fruit. —*Cory*

⊹⊱ BAKING TIME: 20 TO 25 MINUTES / SERVES 8 ⊰⊹

1 tablespoon unsalted butter, at room temperature, for sheet pan

FRUIT

2 dry pints ripe strawberries, hulled and sliced

2 tablespoons granulated sugar

2 teaspoons freshly squeezed lemon juice

SHORTCAKE

2½ cups (12½ ounces) all-purpose flour

2½ teaspoons baking powder

½ cup (2½ ounces) yellow cornmeal

⅔ cup (4½ ounces) granulated sugar, plus ⅓ cup (1¾ ounces) to top shortcakes

1 teaspoon fine sea salt

1½ cups heavy cream

4 teaspoons lemon zest

Preheat the oven to 350°F. Butter a baking sheet.

To prepare the fruit, toss the strawberries in a bowl with the sugar and lemon juice. Mash a small amount of the berries so they release their juice. Place the berries in the refrigerator for 30 minutes to draw out their juices.

While the strawberries are macerating, prepare the shortcake. Mix together the flour, baking powder, cornmeal, sugar, and salt in a bowl, then stir in the cream, lemon zest, and orange zest until just combined. Turn the dough out onto a floured board and form into a ball, then knead 8 to 12 times, or until the dough holds shape (but be careful not to overwork it). Cut the dough into 8 equal portions and roll into balls. Dip each ball into the melted butter, then dip half of the ball into a small bowl with the ⅓ cup sugar. Place each ball on the prepared baking sheet, sugar-side up. Bake for 20 to 25 minutes, or until lightly browned and baked through. Cool on a wire rack.

4 teaspoons orange zest (about
1 large orange)

¼ cup (2 ounces) unsalted butter,
melted

Chantilly cream (page 145),
for serving

While the shortcakes are cooling, make the Chantilly
cream.

To serve, cut the shortcakes in half horizontally. Place
the bottom of the shortcake on a small plate, then ladle
a scoop of juicy berries on the shortcake so the fruit covers
part of the shortcake and cascades down the side onto the
plate. Top the berries with Chantilly cream, and lay the top
of the shortcake biscuit tipped on its side next to the strawberry shortcake. Serve immediately.

Storage: Once assembled, these shortcakes will not keep;
however, if the berries and shortcakes are kept separated,
you may make leftover shortcakes the following day. Store
the shortcake biscuits in an airtight container at room temperature, and keep the strawberries refrigerated.

summer ⚬⚬⚬⚬⚬⚬⚬

I fondly remember my summers as a young boy in the rural Willamette Valley, where I picked and ate blackberries to my heart's content. I used to amble down the road on an August morning to the bramble bushes that grew wild near our house. Trying not to get caught by the thorns, I would peek under the verdant leaves, the dew still wet on the plants, searching for berries that were shiny and black, ripe and sweet. If I got too greedy, I would eat the reddish-purple ones, too, only to immediately regret it as the tart juice made my lips pucker. As the day grew warmer, my stomach grew fuller. After eating my fill, I would return home with stained fingers and a stained face, blissfully content during the dog days of summer.

In summer, many fruits are readily available right outside your door. Himalayan blackberries, for example, grow wild in the Pacific Northwest and make a great pie. Plum trees are heavy with ripe fruit, their branches hanging over the neighbor's fence. Roadside stands pop up in summer, offering local fruit at a good price, often sold by the youngsters who picked the fruit. These just-picked fruits are at the peak of flavor and take little preparation to become a delicious dessert. If you would rather be outside enjoying summer than in your kitchen, try making a Raspberry Fool (page 69) or the Tayberry Oat Buckle (page 77), both of which do not take long to prepare.

In the Willamette Valley, U-pick fields abound in summer, many of them just on the outskirts of town. The strawberry U-pick fields that usher in the season give way to blueberry, raspberry, and boysenberry U-pick fields as summer progresses. Later in the season, fragrant peach U-pick orchards on Sauvie Island and near the Canby Ferry beckon families to come harvest the crop—a fun activity for kids, given the ease of picking a peach. I have always thought that to be fair, those U-pick fields should weigh the children before and after they spend an afternoon in the field picking (and eating) fruit, and adjust the cost of the purchase accordingly!

Portland is fortunate to have many thriving farmers markets, where the local fruit growers feature their fruit at peak season. During the summer months, the abundance of irresistible fruit spilling out of picturesque baskets taunts us to make jam (page 148), bake a Marionberry Pie (page 62), or throw together the Stone Fruit Tea Cake (page 52) for a picnic. What a difference in flavor when you pick fruit at the peak of its season! Here are some tips on what to keep in mind when selecting summer fruit.

BLUEBERRIES

Pick firm, smooth fruit that is not wrinkled (a sign of aging). Size will vary according to variety, but color is a good indicator of ripeness: blueberries should be a deep purple-blue, not reddish, in color. Like cane berries, check under the top layer in a basket of berries to make sure no berries below are withered or crushed. Blueberries should be ripe when you buy them, as they will not continue to ripen. Keep blueberries refrigerated, unwashed and covered. Any moisture will hasten their deterioration, so do not wash them before refrigerating. If freshly picked, they should last for up to two weeks.

CURRANTS

At their peak, fresh currants are mouth-puckeringly sour in a good way. What's more, red currants are visually stunning in any dessert. Red, white, and pink currants have round, shiny, translucent berries, while black currants are a matte blackish purple. The best way to know if currants are ripe is to try them. Avoid currants that look like they have been off the vine for a while; brown stems and wrinkled skin are dead giveaways. Stored in a sealed container in the refrigerator, currants will keep for up to one week.

PEACHES, NECTARINES, AND APRICOTS

Put the fruit to your nose: an intoxicating fragrant aroma indicates ripe fruit. Smooth, unblemished skin is also a good sign for stone fruit; avoid any with bruises or brown spots. Although an orange-rose blush is enticing, do not go by color alone to choose your fruit, as different varieties mature to different colors when they ripen. Pick fruits that are heavy for their size, a sign that the fruit is juicy. Ripe fruit will yield a bit to the touch but should not feel mushy. Never refrigerate stone fruit until it is ripe, and enjoy it within a few days.

PLUMS

Plums should be firm. Be cautious if they look like water balloons, as they are probably past their peak. Color is not an indicator of ripeness; plums come in every color imaginable. For example, Shiro plums are bright yellow, Santa Rosa plums are a crimson red, and Italian prune plums (also called Empress plums) are a beautiful bluish purple. Avoid plums that look bruised or discolored or that have soft spots or shriveled skin. A dull white film on the skin, sometimes called bloom, is harmless; it is just nature's way of waterproofing the surface. Ripe plums yield to gentle pressure. Firm plums can be ripened at home in a paper bag. Because each variety varies in sweetness and juice content, the best way to choose which variety to buy is to ask if you can sample them. Refrigerate ripe plums in a bag or loosely covered with plastic wrap and use them within three days.

PLUOTS

Keep your eyes out for oh-so-sweet pluots, a cross between an apricot (three-quarters) and a plum (one-quarter). Pluots look like plums with speckled skin and are sometimes called "dinosaur eggs" due to their appearance. Where you find pluots, you might also find **apriums** (also three-quarters apricot, one-quarter plum, but similar to an apricot on the outside) and **plumcots** (half apricot, half plum, they smell like an apricot but taste like a plum). All of these hybrid fruits should be firm and juicy. Like plums, refrigerate ripe pluots in a bag or loosely covered with plastic wrap and use them within three days.

RASPBERRIES, BLACKBERRIES, BOYSENBERRIES, AND OTHER CANE BERRIES

More than fifty varieties of berries are grown in Oregon. In addition to red raspberries and blackberries, you will find black raspberries (also called "black caps"), boysenberries (a reddish purple blackberry with a hint of raspberry), Olallieberries (a cultivated berry that is two-thirds blackberry and one-third raspberry), Marion-berries (another blackberry cultivar, named after the county in which it was tested), loganberries (a cross between a blackberry and a red raspberry), tayberries, and many other cultivated varieties, all with unique and delectable flavors. Berries are fragile and age quickly after being picked; check carefully under the top layer of berries in a basket to ensure that the berries underneath are not crushed or moldy. If you are picking the berries yourself, place them gently into a flat and avoid layering them too high or you will meet disappointment later, when you find those at the bottom crushed. Berries should be plump and shiny; if they are watery, wrinkled, or dull, they may be past their prime. Refrigerate berries and use them as soon as possible. They do not last long once picked.

raspberry red currant cobbler

Oregon is a dominant grower of red raspberries in the United States. Many varieties are named for areas in the Willamette Valley, such as Amity, Canby, and Willamette. Meeker, another popular variety, is available throughout the country. These varieties appear in mid-June and are available for about a month, then many of them reappear for a second season during August and into September. The first crop tends to have the most pectin, creating a thicker consistency when cooked. The addition of red currants, an emerging fruit crop in Oregon, lends tartness to this recipe. Be sure to thoroughly remove currant stems (see the Kitchen Hint below), which impart an unwelcome bitter taste when cooked. This recipe uses a rolled biscuit that is a little stiffer in consistency than a drop biscuit, allowing the fruit to bubble up between the dough as it bakes and sets. The buttermilk in the biscuits, which is traditional in my native New England, adds a little zing to this cobbler. —*Julie*

+≡≡ **BAKING TIME: 50 TO 55 MINUTES / SERVES 8 TO 12** ≡≡+

CONTINUED

KITCHEN HINT:

Removing Currant Stems

If the delicate green stems or "strigs" on fresh currants are left on, they will cause an unpleasant bitter taste. To easily pull the currants off their stems, place the currants in the freezer overnight. (They can actually sit on their stems in the freezer for up to 4 weeks.) Once the currants are frozen, roll them between your hands or over a mesh screen to separate the fruit from the stems without crushing the currants. They will defrost as you do this, so work with small batches and be ready to bake with your currants once they are destemmed.

1 tablespoon unsalted butter,
at room temperature, for dish

FRUIT FILLING

1½ cups (10½ ounces)
granulated sugar

2 tablespoons cornstarch

1 teaspoon ground cinnamon

½ teaspoon fine sea salt

3 dry pints (6 cups) raspberries,
fresh or frozen

1 dry pint (2 cups) red currants,
fresh or frozen

2 tablespoons pure vanilla extract

BISCUIT

2 cups (10 ounces) all-purpose flour

3 tablespoons granulated sugar
plus 1 tablespoon to top biscuits

1 teaspoon baking powder

1 teaspoon fine sea salt

¾ cup (6 ounces) cold unsalted
butter, cut into small cubes

¾ cup plus 1 tablespoon cold
buttermilk

Preheat the oven to 375°F. Butter a 3-quart baking dish.

To make the fruit filling, rub the sugar, cornstarch, cinnamon, and salt together in a large bowl. Add the raspberries and currants and toss to combine, then gently stir in the vanilla. Spoon the fruit into the prepared pan, being sure to scrape the bowl well.

To make the biscuit, whisk the flour, 3 tablespoons of the sugar, the baking powder, and salt together in a bowl. Add the butter and toss until evenly coated. Using your fingertips or a pastry blender, cut in the butter until the size of large peas. (Alternatively, you can put the dry ingredients in a food processor and pulse to combine. Add the butter and pulse until the butter is the size of large peas, then transfer to a bowl.) Pour in the ¾ cup buttermilk and stir just until the dry ingredients are moistened. The dough will be crumbly, with large pieces of butter still visible.

Turn the dough out onto a lightly floured work surface and gently press the dough together to form a rectangle, then roll out to a thickness of ⅓ inch. Cut out twelve 2½-inch round or square biscuits, rerolling the scraps as needed. Place biscuits atop the filling, then brush the tops of the biscuits with the 1 tablespoon buttermilk and sprinkle with the remaining 1 tablespoon sugar.

Bake for 50 to 55 minutes, or until the biscuits are golden and the filling is bubbling all over. Serve warm.

Storage: This cobbler is best if eaten the day it is made. Any leftovers can be covered with a tea towel to be finished for breakfast. Reheat in a 300°F oven until warmed through.

double-crusted pluot crisp

This recipe is a crisp lover's delight: the topping is not only crumbled over the top of the fruit, it is also spread as the base of the dish. Pluots are a cross between an apricot and a plum, but the sugar content of a pluot is much higher than that of any ordinary plum or apricot, yielding fruit of incomparable sweetness. The fruit looks like a plum on the outside, and just like plums, they come in many colors and sizes. A popular variety is Dapple Dandy; its skin is greenish yellow with red spots, turning maroon dappled with yellow as it matures. Flavor Grenade and Flavor King are two other wonderful varieties. Pluots are available in late summer and early fall, with different varieties appearing at different times of the season. For this recipe, feel free to mix and match any varieties you find at the peak of ripeness.

⊹≈ **BAKING TIME: 60 MINUTES / SERVES 8 TO 10** ≈⊹

CRISP

1⅓ cups (7 ounces) all-purpose flour

1 cup (3½ ounces) rolled oats

¾ cup packed (5¾ ounces) brown sugar

1 teaspoon ground cinnamon

½ teaspoon fine sea salt

10 tablespoons (5 ounces) unsalted butter, melted

FRUIT FILLING

½ cup (3½ ounces) granulated sugar

1 tablespoon cornstarch

Pinch of fine sea salt

8 pluots, thinly sliced (6 cups prepped)

Juice of 1 lemon

1 teaspoon pure vanilla extract

Preheat the oven to 350°F.

To make the crisp, mix the flour, oats, brown sugar, cinnamon, and salt together in a bowl, then stir in the melted butter. Press a little more than half of the mixture into the bottom of a 9-inch square baking pan.

To make the fruit filling, rub the granulated sugar, cornstarch, and salt together in a large bowl, then add the pluots, lemon juice, and vanilla and toss to combine.

Spread the fruit evenly over the bottom layer of the crisp, then sprinkle the remaining crisp on top. Bake in the middle of the oven for 60 minutes, or until the crisp is golden and the fruit bubbles up through the topping. Cool for 20 minutes before serving.

Storage: Wrapped in plastic wrap, any leftovers will keep at room temperature for up to 3 days. Rewarm in a 300°F oven until heated through.

raspberry cream brown betty

At Baker & Spice, we use challah and country white bread for this recipe. Our preference is challah, because it lends a rich consistency to the recipe due to its high egg content. If using challah (or brioche) omit the 2 tablespoons sugar when preparing the bread cubes. The pastry cream, which you can make in advance, will be thinner than a classic version but will thicken into a custard during the baking process, creating a dessert with the consistency of bread pudding. Baking in ramekins allows the betty to bake quickly so that the berries retain their natural character.

┼━ BAKING TIME: 30 MINUTES / SERVES 6 ━┼

1 tablespoon unsalted butter, at room temperature, for dishes

3 cups small (¼-inch) bread cubes

¼ cup (2 ounces) unsalted butter, melted

2 tablespoons granulated sugar (only if not using challah or brioche)

PASTRY CREAM

Seeds scraped from ½ vanilla bean

2 cups half-and-half

⅔ cup (4½ ounces) granulated sugar

½ teaspoon fine sea salt

6 egg yolks

1 tablespoon cornstarch

½ dry pint (1 cup) raspberries

SEE HINT: "VANILLA BEANS" PAGE 20

Preheat the oven to 350°F. Butter six 5-ounce ramekins.

Spread the bread cubes in a single layer on a baking sheet and bake for 15 minutes. Once the bread is cool, toss it with the melted butter and sugar (if using). Set aside.

To make the pastry cream, put the vanilla bean seeds in to a saucepan. Add the half-and-half and vanilla pod and cook over medium-low heat until hot but not boiling. Separately, whisk the sugar and salt into the egg yolks and continue whisking until slightly thickened and lighter in color. Add the cornstarch and whisk until combined. Slowly pour half of the hot liquid into the yolk mixture, stirring constantly until well blended. Pour the yolk mixture into the saucepan and cook over medium heat, whisking constantly, until the mixture begins to thicken and bubble. Strain the mixture through a fine-mesh sieve and stir frequently until cool.

Distribute half of the bread cubes among the prepared ramekins. Pour the pastry cream over the bread cubes, then put the berries atop the pastry cream. Top with the remaining bread cubes. Bake for 15 minutes, or until the tops have browned and the berries bleed slightly. Cool to room temperature.

Storage: This dessert should be eaten as soon as it is cooked, but any leftovers can be covered with plastic wrap and stored in the refrigerator overnight. Reheat at 325°F for about 10 minutes, until warmed through.

stone fruit tea cake

Tea cake is not overly sweet and tastes great as an afternoon treat paired with hot tea (hence its name) or coffee. Here, a shortbread-style dough encloses the fruit. This recipe bakes well using frozen fruit simply sprinkled with raw turbinado sugar on top of the dough. You might want to bake a double batch of the dough; since it keeps so well in the freezer, you can pull it out to use on short notice anytime you have lots of any fruit on hand. This cake is delicious served with a dollop of Chantilly cream (page 145).

✦ BAKING TIME: 30 TO 40 MINUTES / SERVES 10 TO 12 ✦

1 tablespoon unsalted butter, at room temperature, for pan

2¼ cups (11¼ ounces) all-purpose flour

1 teaspoon baking powder

1 teaspoon fine sea salt

1 cup (7 ounces) granulated sugar

¾ cup (6 ounces) unsalted butter, at room temperature

3 eggs

1 tablespoon pure vanilla extract

2½ cups coarsely chopped mixed stone fruit, fresh or frozen

1 tablespoon turbinado sugar

Whisk the flour, baking powder, and salt together in a bowl. Using a handheld mixer with beaters or a stand mixer with the paddle attachment, cream the sugar and butter together on medium-high speed for 3 to 5 minutes, until light and fluffy. Add the eggs one at a time, scraping down the sides of the bowl after each addition, then stir in the vanilla. Add the flour mixture and stir just until a smooth dough forms. Wrap the dough in plastic wrap, flatten into a 1-inch-thick disk, and freeze for 30 minutes.

Preheat the oven to 375°F. Butter a shallow 10-inch round baking pan or tart pan.

Divide the dough into two equal portions and pat one portion evenly into the bottom of the prepared pan. Spread the fruit over the dough. Break the remainder of the dough into tablespoon-size pieces and distribute atop the fruit, then sprinkle the turbinado sugar over the dessert.

Bake for 30 to 40 minutes, or until lightly golden and firm. Cool for 30 minutes before serving.

Storage: Wrapped in plastic wrap, this tea cake will keep at room temperature for up to 3 days. You can also freeze the unbaked dough; if wrapped well, it will keep for up to 3 months. You can freeze a whole, unbaked cake with fruit (again, wrapped well) for 1 month.

apricot raspberry cobbler

There are two types of people in this world: those who like pie and those who prefer cobbler. This recipe is a dream for those in the latter group. This cakelike cobbler has all the best parts of the dessert, from the chewiness of the cobbler dough to the sweet, juicy cooked fruit. For this recipe, you will spread the cobbler batter onto the bottom of a pan then layer the fruit on top. As the dessert bakes, the batter will rise up into the fruit. For the apricots, Blenheims are divine, but Pattersons, Tiltons, and Castlebrites would also work well.

⊹═══ BAKING TIME: 45 MINUTES / SERVES 8 TO 10 ═══⊹

1 tablespoon unsalted butter, at room temperature, for dish

FRUIT FILLING

10 apricots, pitted and each sliced into 8 to 10 pieces (1½ pounds prepped)

1 dry pint (2 cups) raspberries, fresh or frozen

¾ cup (5¼ ounces) granulated sugar

½ teaspoon fine sea salt

BATTER

1½ cups (7½ ounces) all-purpose flour

2 teaspoons baking powder

½ teaspoon fine sea salt

6 tablespoons (3 ounces) unsalted butter, at room temperature

¾ cup (5 ounces) granulated sugar

¾ cup whole milk

1 tablespoon turbinado sugar

Preheat the oven to 375°F. Butter a 2-quart baking dish.

To make the fruit filling, toss the apricots and raspberries with the sugar and salt in a bowl and set aside to draw out some of the juices while you prepare the batter.

To make the batter, sift together the flour, baking powder, and salt in a bowl. Using a handheld mixer with beaters or a stand mixer with the paddle attachment, cream the butter and granulated sugar together on medium-high speed for 3 to 5 minutes, until light and fluffy. Stir in the flour mixture in three additions alternating with the milk in two additions, beginning and ending with the dry ingredients and scraping down the sides of the bowl occasionally.

Spread the batter evenly in the prepared pan and distribute the fruit over the batter, being sure to scrape the bowl well. Sprinkle the turbinado sugar over the top.

Bake in the bottom third of the oven for about 45 minutes, or until the center of the cake springs back when lightly touched. Cool 20 to 30 minutes before serving.

Storage: This cobbler is best if eaten the day it is made. Any leftovers can be covered with a tea towel to be finished for breakfast. Reheat in a 300°F oven until warmed through.

nectarine, boysenberry, and almond crisp

Nectarines are too often overlooked in summer, possibly because they get upstaged by peaches, which ripen at the same time. A nectarine's characteristics are similar to a peach, but nectarines are glabrous (that is, their skin lacks the downy fuzz found on peaches). Nectarines have a high water content, and they release a great deal of moisture as they bake. Because boysenberries also have a high water content, cornstarch is added to the filling of this crisp to compensate for the moisture. You will want to use a wide dish for this recipe so the filling can spread out in a shallow layer, which allows more water to evaporate. Almonds are our first choice to complement the combination of nectarines and boysenberries, but walnuts or hazelnuts also work well.

BAKING TIME: 45 TO 55 MINUTES / SERVES 8 TO 10

1 tablespoon unsalted butter, at room temperature, for dish

CRISP TOPPING

1¼ cups (6¼ ounces) all-purpose flour

¾ cup (5¼ ounces) granulated sugar

1 teaspoon fine sea salt

½ cup (4 ounces) cold unsalted butter, cut into 6 cubes

¾ cup (3 ounces) sliced almonds, toasted

SEE HINT: "TOASTING NUTS" PAGE 101

Preheat the oven to 400°F. Butter a 3-quart baking dish.

To make the crisp topping, mix the flour, sugar, and salt together in a bowl. Add the butter and toss until evenly coated. Using your fingertips or a pastry blender, cut in the butter until the mixture resembles crumbs. (Alternatively, you can put the dry ingredients in a food processor and pulse to combine. Add the butter and pulse until crumbly, then transfer to a bowl and squeeze the mixture between your fingers to make crumbs.) Add the almonds and mix gently; try not to break the almond slices. Put the topping in the freezer while you prepare the fruit filling.

CONTINUED

nectarine, boysenberry, and almond crisp, continued

FRUIT FILLING

½ cup (5¼ ounces) granulated sugar

2 tablespoons cornstarch

½ teaspoon fine sea salt

6 nectarines, each cut into 10 to 12 slices (3 pounds prepped)

1 dry pint (2 cups) boysenberries

1 tablespoon pure vanilla extract

Vanilla Bean Ice Cream (page 146) or Chantilly cream (page 145), for serving (optional)

To make the fruit filling, rub the sugar, cornstarch, and salt together in a large bowl. Add the nectarines and boysenberries, toss until evenly coated, then gently stir in the vanilla.

Pour the fruit into the prepared baking dish and scatter the topping over the fruit. Bake for 45 to 55 minutes, or until the topping is golden and the fruit is bubbling. Cool for 30 minutes before serving, topped with Vanilla Bean Ice Cream or Chantilly cream.

Storage: Wrapped in plastic wrap, the crisp will keep at room temperature for up to 3 days. Reheat in a 325°F oven for 10 minutes before serving.

lemon blueberry buckle

Blueberries are the ideal fruit to use in a buckle because they sink into the cake batter yet retain their integrity while baking. Numerous varieties are grown in Oregon—at last count, they numbered close to twenty. The season is constantly expanding and currently runs from June until October. The varieties track the season, with the Atlantic, Burlington, Concord, Dixie, Pemberton, and Berkeley offering succulent berries over the expanse of summer. If you are fortunate enough to have the opportunity to taste different varieties side-by-side, you will be able to detect significant variations in sugar content, acidity and skin texture.

My mother, Cheryl, clipped this recipe from the paper in Burlington, Vermont, in the 1980s, and it has been a well-loved classic in my family ever since. The combination of lemon and buttermilk gives this buckle a zesty edge. —*Julie*

⊹⤝ BAKING TIME: 45 TO 50 MINUTES / SERVES 6 TO 8 ⤞⊹

1 tablespoon unsalted butter, at room temperature, for pan

CRUMB TOPPING

½ cup (2½ ounces) all-purpose flour

⅓ cup (2¼ ounces) granulated sugar

⅛ teaspoon fine sea salt

Zest of 1 lemon

¼ cup (2 ounces) unsalted butter, at room temperature, cubed

SEE HINT: "ZESTING CITRUS" PAGE 134

Preheat the oven to 350°F. Butter a 9-inch square baking pan.

To make the crumb topping, mix the flour, sugar, salt, and lemon zest together in a bowl, then add the butter and use a fork or your fingers to cut in the butter until the size of peas. Place the topping in the freezer while you mix the cake batter.

To make the cake, whisk the flour, baking powder, baking soda, salt, and nutmeg together in a bowl. Using a handheld mixer with beaters or a stand mixer with the paddle attachment, cream the butter, sugar, and lemon zest together on medium-high speed for 3 to 5 minutes, until light and fluffy. Add the eggs one at a time, scraping down the sides of the bowl after each addition. Stir in the flour mixture in three additions alternating with the buttermilk in two additions, beginning and ending with the dry ingredients and scraping down the sides of the bowl occasionally. Gently fold in 1 cup of the blueberries, spread the batter into the prepared pan, and distribute the remaining 1 cup blueberries over the cake.

CAKE

1 1/2 cups plus 2 tablespoons
(8 1/4 ounces) all-purpose flour

1 teaspoon baking powder

1/4 teaspoon baking soda

1/2 teaspoon fine sea salt

1/4 teaspoon freshly grated nutmeg

6 tablespoons (3 ounces) unsalted
butter, at room temperature

3/4 cup (5 1/4 ounces) granulated sugar

Zest of 1 lemon

2 eggs

1/2 cup buttermilk

2 cups (10 ounces) blueberries,
fresh or frozen

LEMON SYRUP

1/3 cup (2 1/4 ounces) granulated sugar

Juice of 2 lemons

Sprinkle the chilled crumb topping over the berries, then bake for 45 to 50 minutes, or until lightly golden and firm on top.

To make the glaze, combine the sugar and lemon juice in a small saucepan and whisk until blended. Cook over medium-low heat, stirring occasionally, for 8 to 10 minutes, until syrupy. The glaze will bubble while cooking, so you may need to remove it from the heat to check that it is thick enough.

Pour the glaze over the cake as soon as it is removed from the oven. Reheat the syrup briefly if it has become too thick to pour.

Storage: Covered in plastic wrap, the buckle will keep at room temperature for 2 to 3 days.

vanilla-spiked plum galette

My house has fruit trees tucked away into one corner of the yard. After ten years and very little attention from me, the trees remain prolific, especially the plums I often forget about until late summer, when the tree is covered with beautiful chartreuse-tinged red orbs. It is a stunning display. The plums end up at the bakery, where they become tarts or jam, or a rustic galette infused with the essence of vanilla, as in this recipe. —*Julie*

⇥ BAKING TIME: 50 TO 55 MINUTES / SERVES 8 TO 10 ⇤

1 recipe Galette Dough (page 153)

¾ cup (5¼ ounces) granulated sugar

Seeds scraped from ½ vanilla bean

1 tablespoon cornstarch

½ teaspoon fine sea salt

6 plums, pitted and each cut into eighths (1½ pounds prepped)

Crème fraîche (page 146), for serving

Line a baking sheet with parchment paper or grease it generously with cooking spray. Roll the dough into a 13- to 14-inch circle, then transfer to the prepared baking sheet. It should overhang the sheet a bit.

Rub the sugar and vanilla bean seeds together in a bowl, then rub in the cornstarch and salt. Sprinkle 2 tablespoons of the mixture over the dough, leaving a 2-inch border around the edge. Toss the plums with the remaining sugar mixture. The plums will begin to release their juices, so lift each slice from the juice and arrange the slices on the dough, skin side down, in a spiral beginning 2 inches from the outside edge and ending in the center. Drizzle the plum juices over the fruit. Fold the outer edge of the dough over the outermost plums, pleating the dough as necessary.

Position a rack in the lower third of the oven and preheat the oven to 400°F. Put the galette in the refrigerator for 20 minutes to chill and relax the dough.

Bake the galette in the lower third of the oven for 30 minutes, then turn the oven down to 350°F and bake for an additional 20 to 25 minutes, or until the crust is golden and the fruit is bubbling. Check the galette toward the end of the cooking time. If the crust is getting a bit dark, loosely cover it with aluminum foil. Cool for 30 minutes before serving, topped with a small dollop of crème fraîche.

Storage: Covered with a tea towel, the galette will keep at room temperature for up to 2 days.

marionberry pie

Marionberries are a cross between Chehalem and Olallie blackberries. They are named after Marion County, Oregon, where they were first extensively grown. Marionberries have an aromatic bouquet and an intense blackberry flavor. They are usually quite tart (as a result, this recipe does not call for any lemon juice). The large, not-too-seedy berry is perfect for a pie. My wife, Joy, had an aunt who loved to bake pies, and the end of summer was always marked by family dinners with Marionberry pie. If you do not have access to Marionberries, any other blackberry would work for this recipe—in addition to your basic blackberry, look for boysenberries, youngberries, silvanberries, loganberries, or Olallieberries. —*Cory*

+═══ **BAKING TIME: 60 TO 70 MINUTES / SERVES 8 TO 10** ═══+

½ recipe (2 disks) All-Butter Pie Pastry (page 151)

¾ cup (5¼ ounces) granulated sugar

3½ tablespoons cornstarch

¼ teaspoon fine sea salt

2 dry pints (5 cups) Marionberries, fresh or frozen

1 tablespoon pure vanilla extract

2 tablespoons cold unsalted butter, cut into small cubes

Rub the sugar, cornstarch, and salt together in a large bowl, then add the berries and toss until evenly coated. Gently add the vanilla. Set aside for 15 minutes to draw out some of the juices.

Roll out 1 disk of the pastry and place it in a 9-inch deep-dish pie pan. Dock the dough with a fork 30 to 40 times, then pour in the berry mixture. Dot the butter atop the fruit. Roll the second disk of pastry into a 12-inch square, then cut it into 1-inch strips to make a lattice topping. Lay half of the strips over the top of the pie, then interweave the remaining strips diagonally with the first set of strips. Trim away any excess, then chill the pie for 1 hour.

Preheat the oven to 400°F and position an oven rack in the bottom third of the oven.

Put the pie on a baking sheet to catch any drips, place a crust shield over the pie (see Three Tips for Perfection, page 150), and bake for 60 to 70 minutes, or until the juices of the pie are thick and bubbling. Check the pie after 45 minutes and cover with aluminum foil if it is getting too dark. Cool for 3 hours to let the filling set.

Storage: Covered with a tea towel, the pie will keep at room temperature for up to 3 days.

blueberry cobbler with cornmeal biscuit

The name "cobbler" may come from the phrase "to cobble up," meaning to put together hastily. You can cobble up this dessert if you have blueberries and cornmeal, and it is easy to mix by hand. The flavors of blueberries and cornmeal go well together, and the colors are a knockout when this cobbler is served outdoors on a summer evening.

BAKING TIME: 45 MINUTES / SERVES 8

1 tablespoon unsalted butter, at room temperature, for dish

FRUIT FILLING

¾ cup (5¼ ounces) granulated sugar

3 tablespoons cornstarch

½ teaspoon fine sea salt

3 dry pints (6½ cups or 2 pounds) blueberries, fresh or frozen

2 tablespoons freshly squeezed lemon juice (about ½ lemon)

BISCUIT

1¼ cups (6¼ ounces) all-purpose flour

½ cup (2½ ounces) fine cornmeal

2 tablespoons granulated sugar

1 teaspoon baking powder

½ teaspoon fine sea salt

½ cup (4 ounces) cold unsalted butter, cut into small cubes

1 cup cold heavy cream

4 teaspoons turbinado sugar

Preheat the oven to 375°F. Butter a 2-quart baking dish.

To make the fruit filling, rub the sugar, cornstarch, and salt together in a large bowl. Add the blueberries and toss to combine, then gently stir in the lemon juice. Spoon the fruit mixture into the prepared pan, being sure to scrape the bowl well.

To make the biscuit, whisk the flour, cornmeal, sugar, baking powder, and salt together in a bowl. Add the butter and toss until evenly coated. Using your fingertips or a pastry blender, cut in the butter until the size of peas. Pour in the cream and stir just until the mixture comes together.

Divide the dough into 8 pieces and pat each piece into a 3-inch biscuit. Evenly distribute the biscuits atop the fruit filling, then sprinkle ½ teaspoon of the turbinado sugar on each biscuit.

Bake for about 45 minutes, or until the biscuits are golden and the filling is bubbling in the middle. Serve warm.

Storage: This cobbler is best if eaten the day it is made. Covered with a tea towel, any leftovers will keep at room temperature for up to 3 days.

gingered peach and blackberry pandowdy

This pandowdy recipe is baked with a pastry crust only on top, while the peaches and blackberries thicken and bake together under the crust. This recipe also calls for leaving the skins on the peaches so that they impart their flavor and natural color. During late July and early August, both peaches and blackberries are available, allowing for this delectable combination. Any blackberry will work in this recipe, but Chester blackberries are our favorite for their shiny midnight black color and plump juiciness. These thornless blackberries have a late, long season in western Oregon that can often extend into September. Julie loves them so much she named her cat Chester.

+≈ BAKING TIME: 50 MINUTES / SERVES 8 TO 10 ≈+

1 tablespoon unsalted butter, at room temperature, for dish

¼ recipe (1 disk) All-Butter Pie Pastry (page 151)

4 peaches, pitted (2 pounds prepped)

½ cup (3½ ounces) granulated sugar

Juice of 1 large lemon

2 tablespoons cornstarch

2 tablespoons (½ ounce) chopped candied ginger

½ teaspoon ground ginger

½ teaspoon fine sea salt

1 dry pint (2 cups) blackberries, preferably Chester, fresh or frozen

Preheat the oven to 425°F. Butter a 9-inch deep-dish pie pan.

Wash the peaches, pierce the skins all over with a fork, then slice each peach into 10 to 12 slices, depending on the size of the fruit. Put the peaches in a bowl, add the sugar and lemon juice, and toss gently until evenly coated. Set aside for 15 to 20 minutes to draw out some of the juices.

Strain the peach juice into a small saucepan over medium heat and cook, stirring occasionally, until reduced by half. Rub the cornstarch, candied ginger, ground ginger, and salt together in a bowl.

Roll the pie pastry out a little larger than the diameter of your pie pan. Place the pie pan upside-down atop the pastry and use it to cut the pastry to size.

Add the cornstarch mixture and reduced juice to the peaches, add the blackberries, and stir gently until evenly combined. Pour into the prepared pan and top with the pastry circle. If the crust is a bit larger than the pan, tuck it inside the pan. Place the pie on a baking sheet to collect any drips.

Vanilla Bean Ice Cream (page 146), for serving

Bake for 50 minutes, or until the crust is golden and the fruit is bubbling. Cool for 1 hour before serving, topped with a scoop of Vanilla Bean Ice Cream.

Storage: This dessert should be eaten soon after it is made, but any leftovers can be covered with a tea towel and stored at room temperature until the next morning, when they will make a delicious breakfast.

stone fruit slump

A slump is a simple steamed pudding, somewhat akin to a cobbler, that uses whatever fruit you have on hand. Unlike most of the other recipes in this book, a slump is usually cooked on the top of the stove; first you heat the fruit, then you top it with dumplings and simmer the slump to perfection. This is a perfect dessert to make on a hot day, as you will not need to turn on your oven. The amount of sugar needed in the fruit filling will vary depending on the sweetness of the fruit. It is important to choose a pot with a tight-fitting lid, so the dumplings will cook through.

 **SERVES 8**

FRUIT FILLING

4½ pounds mixed plums, nectarines, or peaches, fresh or frozen, pitted (8 to 9 cups or 3 pounds prepped)

¾ to 1 cup (5¼ to 7 ounces) granulated sugar

3 tablespoons cornstarch

½ teaspoon fine sea salt

2 tablespoons freshly squeezed lemon juice (about ½ lemon)

To make the fruit filling, slice the fruit over a bowl so you can collect all of the juices. Slice each fruit into 10 to 12 pieces, depending on the size of the fruit, and drop the slices into the bowl. Separately, rub the sugar, cornstarch, and salt together in a small bowl, then add to the fruit and gently toss to coat. Gently stir in the lemon juice, then scrape the fruit and juices into a 10- to 12-inch nonreactive, deep skillet or a wide 5-quart saucepan or Dutch oven. Whatever pan you choose, it must have a tight-fitting lid. Let stand for 15 minutes. During this time, the fruit will release some of its juices and the sugar will begin to dissolve.

Bring the fruit mixture to a low simmer over medium-low heat. You will need to stir occasionally to prevent the juice from sticking to the bottom of the pan, but do so gently to avoid breaking down the pieces of fruit. Simmer for about 2 minutes, until slightly thickened. Remove from the heat.

CONTINUED

DUMPLINGS

1 cup (5 ounces) all-purpose flour

½ cup unsifted (2½ ounces) cake flour

2 tablespoons granulated sugar

1 teaspoon baking powder

½ teaspoon baking soda

½ teaspoon fine sea salt

½ teaspoon ground cinnamon

½ teaspoon ground cardamom

½ cup (4 ounces) cold unsalted butter, cut into ½-inch cubes

1 cup cold buttermilk

To make the dumplings, whisk the flours, sugar, baking powder, baking soda, salt, cinnamon, and cardamom together in a bowl. Add the butter and toss until evenly coated. Using your fingertips or a pastry blender, cut in the butter until the size of peas. Add the buttermilk and stir just until the mixture comes together; it will be a slightly wet dough.

In 8 portions, place the dough atop the fruit, distributing the dumplings evenly over the surface. Return to the stovetop and bring to a gentle simmer over low heat. Cover with a tight-fitting lid and continue simmering for 18 to 22 minutes, or until the dumplings are puffy and cooked through to the center. Remove the cover and let cool for 15 minutes before serving.

Storage: Sadly, slumps do not keep well. Eat this one immediately.

KITCHEN HINT:

Peeling a Peach

To peel or not to peel—that is the question! Most folks peel their peaches, but there is no need to peel nectarines or plums. If you want to peel ripe peaches, submerge them in boiling water for 30 seconds, then pull them out; the peel will strip right off. Instead of peeling peaches, try washing them well and then piercing them gently with a fork. Once they are sliced and baked, the peel will fall apart into the fruit and add a rosy color to any dessert.

raspberry fool

This recipe calls for mascarpone, which is a triple-cream cheese (although some swear it is not a cheese at all, just cream with a culture added to create a dairy product that resembles crème fraîche). Many people think of mascarpone only as an ingredient in the Italian dessert tiramisu, but it is great for any creamy dessert, as it is slightly sweet and very smooth. Mascarpone is available in the dairy aisle of most well-stocked grocery stores or at specialty cheese shops. Buy the creamiest version available. Fresh raspberries are a must for this recipe.

 **SERVES 8**

1 dry quart (4 cups) raspberries

1/2 cup plus 3 tablespoons (3 1/2 ounces plus 1 1/4 ounces) granulated sugar

Pinch of fine sea salt

1/4 cup raspberry or orange liqueur, or 2 tablespoons pure vanilla extract

1 cup (9 ounces) cold mascarpone

2 cups cold heavy cream

1/2 teaspoon ground cinnamon

SEE HINT:
"WHIPPING
CREAM"
PAGE 145

Mix 3 1/2 cups of the raspberries, 1/2 cup of the sugar, the salt, and liqueur together in a bowl and use a pastry blender or a fork to mash the berries. Let sit for 20 minutes to draw out some of the juices. Strain half of the berries back into the bowl through a fine-mesh sieve and discard the seeds.

Place a mixing bowl or the bowl of a stand mixer into the freezer for 5 minutes, then put the mascarpone, cream, cinnamon, and the 3 tablespoons sugar in the bowl and mix on low speed using a handheld mixer with beaters or a stand mixer with the whisk attachment. Once the mixture has come together, gradually increase the speed to high and whip just until soft peaks form.

Fold in the raspberry mixture just until combined. Do not worry about incorporating it completely; a few streaks of cream are just fine. Distribute the fool between 8 serving cups and chill for 30 minutes. Garnish with the remaining 1/2 cup raspberries before serving.

Storage: This fool is best served the day it is made. Covered with plastic wrap and stored in the refrigerator, any leftovers will keep for an additional day, but the fool will not look as pretty.

caramel peach grunt

No one knows how this type of dessert, made with cooked fruit and biscuit dough, came to be called a "grunt." Some say it is because you can hear the fruit grunt as the air escapes (just as you can see the dessert buckle or slump). Others say it is because folks grunt with pleasure when they enjoy this dessert. Let's hope not! Regardless of the origin of the name, grunts usually cook on top of the stove. Here, the peaches and caramel cook on the stovetop, but the biscuits go into the oven to crisp up. This is an easy recipe—you do not even need to peel the peaches—and it looks country perfect when prepared in an iron skillet. Use two pot holders (and both hands) when you remove it from the oven, or you will find yourself grunting from the weight of the skillet!

✢ BAKING TIME: 25 TO 30 MINUTES / SERVES 10 TO 12 ✢

8 peaches, skins pierced and each cut into 10 to 12 slices (3 pounds prepped)

½ cup granulated sugar plus 1 cup for caramel (10½ ounces total)

3 tablespoons cornstarch

½ teaspoon fine sea salt

¼ cup water

2 tablespoons unsalted butter

1 tablespoon pure vanilla extract

Gently toss the peaches with ½ cup of the sugar in a large bowl and let sit for 20 to 30 minutes to draw out some of the juices. Strain the juice into a separate bowl. Rub the cornstarch and salt together in a small bowl, add to the peaches, and gently toss to combine.

Position an oven rack in the lower third of the oven and preheat the oven to 375°F.

Combine the remaining 1 cup sugar and the water in a 12-inch cast-iron skillet or other ovenproof skillet over medium-high heat and stir until dissolved. Once the sugar is dissolved, stop stirring and only swirl the pan as necessary to keep the mixture heated evenly. Once the sugar has turned dark amber, remove from the heat and slowly pour in the juice collected from the peaches and the butter; be careful, as the caramel is very hot and will boil up when the liquid is added. Return the pan to the heat and bring back to a boil. Once the caramel boils, stir in the peaches and the vanilla, lower the heat to medium, and cook, stirring occasionally, for 10 to 15 minutes, until the peaches have cooked through.

Meanwhile, make the biscuits. Whisk the flour, sugar, baking soda, and salt together in a bowl. Add the butter and toss until evenly coated. Using your fingertips or a pastry

BISCUIT

2 cups (10 ounces) all-purpose flour

2 tablespoons granulated sugar

1 teaspoon baking soda

½ teaspoon fine sea salt

6 tablespoons (3 ounces) cold unsalted butter, cut into small cubes

1 cup cold buttermilk

blender, cut in the butter until the size of small peas. Pour in the buttermilk and stir with a fork just until the dough barely holds together; it will be wet and sticky.

In 12 portions, each about ¼ cup, drop the biscuits atop the peaches. Bake in the lower third of the oven for 25 to 30 minutes, or until the biscuits are lightly golden and puffy. Cool for 20 minutes before serving.

Storage: This grunt will not keep long; it is best served within 4 hours of being made.

KITCHEN HINT:

Making Caramel

Before you start, make sure there is no hidden debris in the sugar. It is best to scrape away the top layer and scoop from underneath. Dirty sugar can cause the caramel to crystallize. Do not let all these dos and don'ts keep you from enjoying the art of caramel making. It is fun, and practice makes perfect!

- Be sure all of your utensils are very clean. Use a spoon that will not absorb the heat or melt!

- Keep the heat level consistent. Medium-high heat is best.

- Watch the caramel at all times, and do not even think about stepping away from the stove, especially when the caramel starts to show some color.

- Never forget how hot the caramel gets.

- When adding liquid to caramel, always remove the pan from the stove and then add the liquid slowly. The hot caramel will boil up when liquid is added.

- Do not stir once the caramel comes to a boil; swirl the pan. If you stir, the caramel will likely crystallize.

- Use a clean pastry brush dipped in cold water to wash down the sides of the pan. This helps keep the sugar from crystallizing.

stone fruit upside-down cornmeal cake

This beautiful dessert showcases succulent stone fruit (a term referring to peaches, apricots, nectarines, plums, and cherries—any fruit that has a pit, or stone) complemented by crunchy cornmeal. You can make either one large cake, or eight individual cakes in ramekins. The latter makes an elegant end to a summer dinner party. Assemble the desserts up to the baking point before guests arrive, then keep them in the refrigerator and pop them into the oven as you sit down for dinner. Your guests will be delighted with their individual warm cakes.

✦ BAKING TIME: 30 MINUTES FOR INDIVIDUAL CAKES, OR 45 TO 50 MINUTES FOR A 10-INCH SKILLET / SERVES 8 ✦

FRUIT TOPPING

4 small stone fruits, such as apricots, plums, or pluots

¼ cup (2 ounces) unsalted butter, melted

½ cup packed (3¾ ounces) brown sugar

Preheat the oven to 350°F.

Score the skin of the fruits with a few strokes of a knife, then slice them in half and remove the pits.

To prepare the fruit topping for individual cakes, distribute the melted butter among eight 5-ounce ramekins, brushing the butter up onto the sides of the ramekins. Sprinkle 1 tablespoon of the brown sugar in each ramekin, then place half of a stone fruit on top of the sugar, cut side down. Place the ramekins on a baking sheet.

Alternatively, to prepare the fruit topping for a single large cake, melt the butter in a 10-inch cast-iron skillet set over medium heat. Add the brown sugar and stir until the sugar dissolves and blends with butter to form a caramel. Remove from the heat and arrange the fruit halves on top of the caramel, cut side down.

CAKE

1¼ cups (6¼ ounces) all-purpose flour

¾ cup (3¾ ounces) fine cornmeal

1½ teaspoons baking powder

¼ teaspoon baking soda

½ teaspoon fine sea salt

½ cup (4 ounces) unsalted butter, at room temperature

⅔ cup (4½ ounces) granulated sugar

2 eggs

1 teaspoon pure vanilla extract

¾ cup buttermilk

To make the cake, whisk the flour, cornmeal, baking powder, baking soda, and salt together in a bowl. Using a handheld mixer with beaters or a stand mixer with the paddle attachment, cream the butter and sugar together on medium-high speed for 3 to 5 minutes, until light and fluffy. Add the eggs one at a time, scraping down the sides of the bowl after each addition, then stir in the vanilla. Stir in the flour mixture in three additions alternating with the buttermilk in two additions, beginning and ending with the dry ingredients and scraping down the sides of the bowl occasionally.

Distribute the batter evenly among the ramekins (about ¼ cup per cake) on top of the fruit, or transfer all of the batter to the skillet and gently spread it evenly over the fruit. Bake in the middle of the oven for about 30 minutes for individual cakes or 45 minutes for the skillet, or until the center of the cake springs back lightly when touched. Allow the individual cakes to cool for 5 minutes before inverting onto plates; the large cake will need 20 minutes to cool before you flip it over.

Storage: This cake is best if eaten the day it is made, but any leftovers can be covered with plastic wrap and enjoyed the following morning for breakfast.

summer fruit trifle

The trifle is an English dessert that has been around for centuries. Along the way, bakers have formed definite opinions about what should and should not be in a trifle. Everyone agrees that a trifle should be composed of layers of cake, sweetened cream, and fruit—a heavenly trilogy by all counts. The disagreement stems from what type of cake to use (chiffon, ladyfingers, or sponge?); what type of cream (Chantilly, custard, or pastry cream?) and what type of fruit (gooseberries, raspberries, or peaches?). Do not even get them started about what kind of liquor to use. We have found that the only thing you need to keep consistent to make a delicious trifle is to use fruit at the peak of its season. What about everything else? Well, you will just have to experiment and join the controversy!

For the fruit, any summer fruit will do. Good choices include strawberries, red currants, peaches, plums, blueberries, blackberries, or cherries. The only frozen fruit that will work in this recipe is frozen raspberries. Regardless of what ingredients you select, use a deep glass bowl to show off the colors and textures of your layered trifle. You can also use individual glasses for a stunning presentation.

 **SERVES 8 TO 12**

1 Vanilla Chiffon Cake (page 156)

PASTRY CREAM

Seeds scaped from ½ vanilla bean

3 cups half-and-half

¾ cup (5¼ ounces) granulated sugar

½ teaspoon fine sea salt

6 egg yolks

2 tablespoons cornstarch

2 tablespoons unsalted butter

½ cup liquor (your favorite: Cointreau, crème de cassis, brandy, rum, or whatever)

To make the pastry cream, put the vanilla bean seeds into a saucepan. Add the half-and-half and vanilla bean pod and cook over medium-low heat until hot but not boiling. Whisk the sugar and salt into the egg yolks in a large bowl and continue whisking until slightly thickened and lighter in color. Add the cornstarch and whisk to combine. Pour one-third of the hot liquid into the yolk mixture, stirring constantly until well blended. Pour the yolk mixture into the saucepan and cook over medium heat, whisking constantly, until the mixture begins to thicken and bubble. Strain the mixture through a fine-mesh sieve into a bowl, then whisk in the butter. Stir frequently to cool (too much stirring will thin out the consistency, so do not go overboard), then refrigerate for 1 hour, until chilled.

CONTINUED

summer fruit trifle, continued

4 cups (2 recipes) Chantilly cream
(page 145)

6 cups ripe summer fruit in
bite-size pieces

Cut the Vanilla Chiffon Cake into three layers. Brush the liquor of your choice on one side of each layer. Place a layer of cake in the bottom of a serving bowl, trimming as needed so it will fit. Layer one-third of the fruit on top of the cake (saving the best third of the fruit for the top layer). Press the fruit slightly to release its juices into the cake. Spread half of the pastry cream on top of the fruit, then top with one-third of the Chantilly cream. Repeat the layering process: another layer of cake, another one-third of the fruit, the remaining pastry cream, and another one-third of the Chantilly cream. Top with the last layer of cake, then spread the remaining Chantilly cream over the cake and top with the remaining fruit.

Cover with plastic wrap and chill for 1 to 4 hours before serving. This time is important to allow the flavors to marry. Serve chilled, straight from the refrigerator.

Storage: Trifles do not keep. If you have any leftovers, cover with plastic wrap, refrigerate, and consume for a very decadent breakfast the next morning.

tayberry oat buckle

The first time I ate tayberries, I was nineteen years old and sitting outside a pub in Kilkenny, Ireland. I had purchased the berries at the market without knowing what they were, and I had a loaf of soda bread and a pint of Smithwick's to round out my meal. The berries tasted so amazing that I was compelled to double back to the market to learn their name. Thus began my love affair with tayberries, which are a cross between a raspberry and a blackberry, somewhat akin to a loganberry, but better. It turns out tayberries are not Irish; they are Scottish and named after the River Tay in Scotland.

This recipe calls for oat flour, which you can find at many natural food stores and some supermarkets (or see the Sources section for online options). Or you can make it yourself by processing rolled oats in a food processor or blender until very finely ground. —*Julie*

⊬⊨ BAKING TIME: 45 TO 50 MINUTES / SERVES 8 TO 12 ⊨⊬

1 tablespoon unsalted butter, at room temperature, for pan

1½ cups (7½ ounces) all-purpose flour

½ cup (2 ounces) oat flour

1 teaspoon baking powder

½ teaspoon baking soda

½ teaspoon fine sea salt

¾ cup (6 ounces) unsalted butter

1 cup (7 ounces) granulated sugar

2 eggs

1 teaspoon pure vanilla extract

1 cup buttermilk

1 dry pint (2½ cups or 9 ounces) tayberries, fresh or frozen

¼ cup (¾ ounce) rolled oats

2 tablespoons turbinado sugar or medium brown sugar

Preheat the oven to 350°F. Butter a 9-inch square baking pan.

Sift the flours, baking powder, baking soda, and salt together in a bowl. Using a handheld mixer with beaters or a stand mixer with the paddle attachment, cream the butter and granulated sugar together on medium-high speed until light and fluffy. Add the eggs one at a time, scraping down the sides of the bowl after each addition, then stir in the vanilla. Stir in the flour mixture in three additions alternating with the buttermilk in two additions, beginning and ending with the dry ingredients and scraping down the sides of the bowl occasionally.

Fold in half of the tayberries and spread the batter in the prepared pan. Distribute the remaining tayberries over the cake, then sprinkle the oats and turbinado sugar over the top.

Bake for 45 to 50 minutes, or until lightly golden and firm on top.

Storage: Wrapped in plastic wrap, the buckle will keep at room temperature for 2 to 3 days.

fall

After the ever-abundant bounty of summer comes the reprieve of autumn. Fall offers beautiful moments that connect me to nature: the harvest moon low on the horizon, the first frost, apples pressed into fresh cider, the rustle of dry leaves underfoot, and pumpkins—lots and lots of pumpkins.

Autumn is a wonderful time to explore fruits that peak in flavor as the weather grows cold and crisp. The season's progression mirrors the characteristics of the various fruits that ripen in September, October, and November. In the Pacific Northwest, fall arrives gradually, with a beautiful cool day here and a crisp breeze there to gently remind us that summer is winding down. In much the same way, fall fruit begins with the subtle introduction of fragile huckleberries, figs, and grapes. As autumn takes on its characteristic crisp chill and strong gusts of wind blow the leaves off the trees, the autumnal harvest similarly builds to a crescendo of hardier pears and apples, their varieties as endless as the colors of the falling leaves.

I ease myself into fall, enjoying the transition from summer to winter, by eating raw apples in the market in September. (When they first appear in August, it is still too early for me to admit that summer is over and fall is on the horizon, so I pass them by and grab a peach instead.) I hold off on baking my first apple pie until much later, hoping to draw out the season. In early fall, when Indian summer casts its warm glow, I make the elegant Fig and Honey Cream Galette (page 107) or the easy and fast Fig and Mixed-Color Raspberry Crumble (page 96). In these stunning desserts, the fruit is not overcooked, and they both offer a taste reminiscent of summer. In later months, once the evenings are dark and the weather has turned cold and damp, I bake the decadent Upside-Down Pear Chocolate Cake (page 102) or the Pumpkin Custard with Cookie Crumb Crust (page 98). Tucking into either of these definitely takes off the chill.

The crisp fall air and the low, hanging light make mornings a beautiful time to wander in your local farmers market. Here are some tips for selecting fruit at the market in autumn.

APPLES

Apples should be bright and well-colored, with a smooth, shiny skin. Avoid any that are bruised or soft and choose firm ones instead. Aroma may also indicate ripeness and good flavor, although, unfortunately, apples are often picked early to avoid storage loss and shipping damage, in which case they may have no aroma at all. There are many varieties of apples to choose from, and you should not hesitate to ask for a sample if you are in doubt about which to buy. We have made some suggestions in our recipes for certain varieties we like, but do not feel restricted to our preferences if you find an intriguing variety at your farmers market. That said, certain varieties really do yield better results. In order of their appearance at the market, varieties used most frequently for baking include Gravenstein, King of Tompkins County, Cox's Orange Pippin, Jonathan, Golden Delicious, Suncrisp, Jonagold, Stayman Winesap, Belle de Boskoop, Fuji, Macoun, Pink Lady, Granny Smith, Newton Pippin, and Braeburn. For applesauce, Gala and Gravenstein apples both appear early, and McIntosh and Cortland are good picks later on in the season. Pink Pearl apples (usually appearing in September) also make a delicious rosy-pink applesauce. For baked apples, look for Macoun or Northern Spy apples. The skin of these apples is durable and makes an excellent shell when baking whole apples. For other desserts, keep in mind that the texture of the apple skin will not break down much during baking. Also, the skin's color may affect the appearance of the dessert, especially if the skin is very dark red, such as Arkansas Black apples. Peeling the apple allows the fruit to break down and bake into the batter or topping of a recipe. When in doubt, peel the apple. Apples store well in cold temperatures and may get mealy if left at room temperature for too long, so keep them in the refrigerator and try to use them within one week.

FIGS

Figs should be plump and soft but not mushy. Avoid figs that are bruised or falling apart. Figs come in many colors depending on the variety: Calimyrna and Adriatic figs have a golden skin, Brown Turkey and Celeste figs are brownish purple, Kadota figs have an amber skin, and Mission figs are a deep purple. Figs are highly perishable and will not last long at room temperature, but they will keep for several days in the refrigerator.

GRAPES

Look for grapes that are still in healthy clusters, fresh off the vine. Grapes should be plump and blemish free, not split open, brown, or shriveled. You want to buy grapes that look ready to burst with juice when you pop one in your mouth. Grapes come in a variety of colors, from translucent gold, light green, and rosy pink to plum-purple and blue-black. They develop their color before they become ripe and they do not sweeten once they are harvested, so they may look ripe but not have the flavor and sweetness you would expect. For the safest bet, taste a grape before you buy the cluster.

HUCKLEBERRIES

Huckleberries, which grow in the wild, are often confused with blueberries. You can tell the two apart because blueberries have many tiny soft seeds, while huckleberries have ten large seeds. Huckleberries are usually small and, depending on the variety, could be ripe when bright red, deep blue, or dark purple. Pick firm, smooth fruit that is not wrinkled. Keep huckleberries refrigerated, unwashed and covered. If freshly picked, they should last for at least one week.

PEARS

Pears do not ripen successfully on the tree—a lesson I learned as a boy when I tried to raid our orchard and could not understand why the pears were always underripe on the branch! Pears do, however, ripen successfully after you buy them, so allow them to sit at room temperature to achieve their characteristic sweetness. We recommend either a Bartlett (which ripens early in the fall) or a Comice (which ripens later) if you seek a pear that is tender and will bake quickly. Boscs and Anjous are naturally firmer and will take longer to break down when baked. Keep your eye out for Concorde pears, a Bosc-Comice cross that has the sweetness of a Comice and the hint of vanilla characteristic of a Bosc. Look for pears that are bright and fresh (the color varies according to the variety, and only Bartletts change color noticeably as they ripen), and avoid any with bruises or soft spots. Check your pears daily to see if they are ripe by gently pressing near the stem. If the pear gives to gentle pressure, it is probably sweet and juicy on the inside and ready to use for baking. Pears do not keep long once they are ripe, but you can prolong their shelf life for a day or two by placing them in the refrigerator. Pear sauce is an ideal way to use very ripe fruit.

QUINCE

Here's a fruit you will not want to sample at the farmers market in its raw form—it will taste sour and astringent. Once cooked, however, quince's unique flavor is delightful. Look for firm yellow fruit and avoid any quince that are very soft or spotted with mold. Quinces bruise easily, but the marks don't affect the quality or taste. Store the fruit in a plastic bag in the refrigerator for several days and be sure to peel them before using.

FALL RASPBERRIES

All berries are fragile and deteriorate quickly after being picked—especially fall raspberries. Check carefully under the top layer of berries in a basket to ensure that the berries underneath are not crushed or moldy. If you're picking the berries yourself, place them gently into a flat and avoid layering them too high or you will meet disappointment later, when you find those at the bottom crushed. Raspberries should be plump and shiny; if they are watery, wrinkled, or dull, they may be past their prime. Refrigerate raspberries and use them as soon as possible. They do not last long once picked.

apple blackberry pie

Many people consider Gravensteins ideal pie apples, but they do not keep and are only available in season, usually late July and early August. I am still avidly featuring summer fruit when the Gravensteins are ripe, and the apple season is so long that we do not want to jump into it in July. If you are making this recipe after Gravensteins have come and gone, use Belle de Boskoop, King of Tompkins County, Granny Smith, Cameo, Pink Lady, Jonagold, Newton Pippin, or Stayman Winesap apples. —*Julie*

⊰═══ BAKING TIME: 90 MINUTES / SERVES 6 TO 8 ═══⊱

½ recipe (2 disks) All-Butter Pie Pastry (page 151)

3 large apples, peeled, cored, and sliced ¼ to ½ inch thick (1 pound prepped)

⅓ cup packed (2½ ounces) brown sugar

2 tablespoons cold unsalted butter

¼ cup (1¾ ounces) granulated sugar

2½ tablespoons cornstarch

1 teaspoon ground ginger

¼ teaspoon fine sea salt

2 dry pints (4 cups or 1 pound) blackberries, fresh or frozen

1 tablespoon freshly squeezed lemon juice

SEE HINT: "TIPS FOR PIE CRUST" PAGE 150

Combine the apples and brown sugar in a bowl and let sit for 30 minutes to draw out some of the juices.

Roll out 1 disk of the pastry and place it in a 9-inch pie pan. Dock the dough with a fork 30 to 40 times. Roll the second disk into a 10-inch round and put the pastry in the refrigerator to chill.

Strain the juice from the apples into a small sauté pan over low heat, add the butter, and cook, stirring occasionally, until reduced by half. Rub the granulated sugar, cornstarch, ginger, and salt together in a large bowl. Add the blackberries and lemon juice and gently toss to coat. Pour in the reduced juice, add the apples, and toss gently until thoroughly combined.

Pour the filling into the pie shell and top with the second crust. Crimp the edges and cut a steam vent in the top, then chill the pie for 1 hour.

Preheat the oven to 400°F and position the oven rack in the bottom third of your oven. Put the pie on a baking sheet to catch any drips, place a crust shield over the pie (see Three Tips for Perfection on page 150), and bake for 45 minutes. Turn the oven down to 350°F and bake an additional 45 minutes, or until crust is golden and the fruit is bubbling. Cool for 3 hours before serving.

Storage: Covered with a tea towel, the pie will keep at room temperature for up to 3 days.

maple apple dumpling

I am always looking for ways to introduce maple syrup into a recipe. Maple syrup goes hand in hand with apples, so it was not hard to find a place for maple syrup in this recipe. Look for small baking apples that hold their shape when baked, like Pink Lady, Macoun, Newton Pippin, or Suncrisp, to name just a few. —*Julie*

+⫘ BAKING TIME: 45 TO 50 MINUTES / SERVES 6 ⫘+

2 tablespoons unsalted butter, at room temperature, for pan

PASTRY

2 cups (10 ounces) all-purpose flour

2 teaspoons baking powder

1 teaspoon fine sea salt

½ cup (4 ounces) cold unsalted butter

½ cup plus 2 tablespoons cold whole milk, as needed

MAPLE GLAZE

1½ cups water

1 cup Grade B maple syrup

¼ teaspoon ground cinnamon

¼ teaspoon freshly grated nutmeg

6 small apples

2 tablespoons unsalted butter, cut into 6 equal pieces

6 teaspoons granulated sugar

Preheat the oven to 425°F. Generously butter a 9-inch square baking pan or other pan large enough to accommodate 6 whole apples.

To make the pastry, mix the flour, baking powder, and salt together in a bowl. Cut the butter into 1-inch pieces, add to the flour mixture, and toss to evenly coat. Use your fingertips or a pastry blender to cut in the butter until completely broken down into the flour. Add the milk a couple tablespoons at a time, stirring well after each addition to evenly moisten the dough. Add only enough milk for the dough to come together in a relatively dry mass. Gather the dough into a ball, then pat it out into a square. Wrap the dough in plastic wrap and refrigerate while you make the glaze and prep the apples.

To make the maple glaze, combine the water, maple syrup, cinnamon, and nutmeg in a saucepan and simmer over medium heat for 5 minutes.

With an apple corer or paring knife, remove the core from each apple; this is a little easier said than done if you do not have the right tools. If you do not have a corer, just cut the apples in half and take out the core. They will be a little harder to wrap in the pastry, but that is better and safer than struggling with a knife. Put 1 piece of the butter and 1 teaspoon of sugar in the cavity of each apple.

Roll out the pastry on a lightly floured surface to form a rectangle measuring 18 by 12 inches. Cut the pastry into six 6-inch squares, and wrap a square around each apple, gathering the ends of the dough at the bottom of the apple and stretching, tucking, and pinching the dough to entirely

wrap the apple. Put the apples, gathered-dough-end down in the prepared pan, then pour the glaze over the apples.

Bake for 15 minutes, then turn the oven down to 350°F and continue to bake for an additional 30 to 35 minutes, or until the pastry is golden and a knife inserted into an apple meets no resistance. Serve warm with some of the syrup spooned over the top.

Storage: Like so many desserts, these apples are best served the day they are made, but any leftovers can be covered in plastic wrap and kept at room temperature for 2 to 3 days.

KITCHEN HINT:

Maple Syrup Grades

Pure maple syrup is graded on both color and flavor. There are two grades for consumer use: Grade A and Grade B. Grade A syrup is further broken down into three classes: light amber, medium amber, and dark amber. Vermont has its own grading system with a slightly higher standard for product density; to achieve the thicker product, Vermont maple syrup is boiled just a bit longer. Vermont uses a slightly different terminology, as does Canada. For example, Grade A Light Amber syrup is called Fancy Grade in Vermont and No. 1 Extra Light in Canada.

- Grade A Light Amber is very light and has a mild, delicate maple flavor. It is usually made earlier in the season when the weather is colder.

- Grade A Medium Amber is a slightly darker and has a bit more maple flavor. The most popular grade of table syrup, it is usually made midseason, after the days begin to warm a bit.

- Grade A Dark Amber is darker than the other Grade A syrups and has a stronger maple flavor. It is usually made even later in the season, when the days are longer and warmer.

- Grade B is made late in the season and is quite dark. It has a very strong maple flavor with undertones of caramel. Because of its strong flavor, Grade B maple syrup is the best choice for baking.

gingered pear and raspberry pandowdy

The combination of pears and raspberries is a definite palate pleaser. You can use any ripe pears in this recipe; if you use Bartletts, you need not peel them. We jazz up this pandowdy by adding candied ginger to the biscuit dough. The effect is a warm and spicy infusion that makes this rustic dessert a comfort food favorite. When you serve this pandowdy with a scoop of Vanilla Bean Ice Cream on a cold autumn evening, you will have everyone "mmm'ing" and asking for more.

BAKING TIME: 50 MINUTES / SERVES 8

1 tablespoon unsalted butter, at room temperature, for pan

FRUIT FILLING

½ cup (3½ ounces) granulated sugar

2 tablespoons plus 1 teaspoon cornstarch

Pinch of fine sea salt

4 large pears, peeled, cored, and sliced (2 pounds prepped)

1 tablespoon freshly squeezed lemon juice

1 dry pint (2 cups or 9 ounces) raspberries, fresh or frozen

1 tablespoon cold unsalted butter, cut into small pieces

Position a rack in the lower third of the oven and preheat the oven to 400°F. Butter a 9-inch cast-iron skillet or 9-inch deep-dish pie pan.

To make the fruit filling, rub the sugar, cornstarch, and salt together in a large bowl, then add the pears and lemon juice and toss until evenly coated. Gently fold in the raspberries, then transfer the fruit to the prepared pan. Distribute the butter atop the fruit.

CONTINUED

gingered pear and raspberry pandowdy, continued

BISCUIT

1¾ cups (8¾ ounces) all-purpose flour

3 tablespoons plus 1 tablespoon (1¾ ounces) granulated sugar

¾ teaspoon baking powder

½ teaspoon fine sea salt

10 tablespoons (5 ounces) cold unsalted butter, cut into small cubes

⅓ cup (2 ounces) chopped candied ginger

⅔ cup plus 1 tablespoon cold buttermilk

To make the biscuit, whisk the flour, 3 tablespoons of the sugar, the baking powder, and salt together in a bowl. Add the butter and toss until evenly coated. Using your fingertips or a pastry blender, cut in the butter until the size of large peas. (Alternatively, you can put the dry ingredients in a food processor and pulse to combine. Add the butter and pulse until the butter is the size of large peas, then transfer to a bowl.) Stir in the candied ginger, then pour in the ⅔ cup buttermilk and stir just until the dry ingredients are moistened. The dough will be crumbly, with large pieces of butter still visible.

Turn the dough out onto a lightly floured work surface and gently press the dough together, then press it into a 9-inch circle. Carefully place the dough atop the fruit. Brush the dough with the 1 tablespoon buttermilk, then sprinkle with the remaining 1 tablespoon sugar.

Bake in the lower third of the oven for 30 minutes, then turn the oven down to 350°F and bake for an additional 20 minutes or until the pastry is golden and the juices are bubbly and thick. Allow to cool for 30 minutes before serving.

Storage: Covered with a tea towel, this pandowdy will keep at room temperature for up to 3 days.

grape galette

If you can find grapes at your local farmers market when the weather turns crisp and cool, they will be perfect for this galette. (If you only have access to the standard grocery store red or green seedless grapes; this is not the recipe for you.) Feel free to mix colors and varieties of grapes; some are sweeter, some more tart, some taste spicy, and some taste like honey. At one farmers market, we found Interlaken (golden), Canadice (red), Sweet Seduction (white), Venus (black), and Glenora (blue-black). Small, seedless grapes are best for this recipe, but if the only grapes available have seeds, simply cut the grapes in half and remove the seeds (and increase the amount of cornstarch by one tablespoon).

⊣⊨ BAKING TIME: 50 TO 60 MINUTES / SERVES 8 TO 10 ⊨⊢

1 tablespoon unsalted butter, at room temperature, for pan

1 recipe Galette Dough (page 152)

4 cups (1¼ pounds) seedless grapes

½ cup (3½ ounces) granulated sugar

2 tablespoons cornstarch

¼ teaspoon fine sea salt

Juice of ½ lime

2 tablespoons cold unsalted butter, cut into small pieces

1 tablespoon confectioners' sugar (optional)

Lightly butter a 9½-inch fluted tart pan with a removable bottom. Roll the dough into a 13- to 14-inch circle and drape it in the tart pan, allowing the excess pastry to hang over the edges. Chill the pastry while you prepare the filling.

Wash the grapes and remove the stems. Rub the sugar, cornstarch, and salt together in a bowl, then add the grapes and toss to coat. Stir in the lime juice, then pour the filling into the tart pan and spread it out evenly. Distribute the butter over the grapes. Fold the overhanging dough over the outer edge of the filling, pleating the dough as necessary.

Preheat the oven to 400°F and position the oven rack in the lower third of the oven. Put the galette into the refrigerator for 20 minutes to chill and relax the dough.

Place the tart pan on a baking sheet covered with greased parchment paper to catch any filling that overflows. Bake for 50 to 60 minutes, or until the crust is golden and the filling is bubbling.

Cool the galette for 30 minutes. You might need to pop it into a warm oven for 5 minutes in order to easily remove the tart ring from the bottom of the pan. Sift the confectioners' sugar over the galette before serving.

Storage: Covered with a tea towel, the galette will keep at room temperature for up to 2 days.

apple and black currant brown betty

A local farmer from Queener Fruit Farms urged us to include a recipe featuring a combination of fresh black currants and apples. Once we tasted this betty, we knew why she made such a delicious suggestion. Many cooks are familiar with black currants in jam or jelly, or perhaps crème de cassis, but not as many people bake with currants—and they should! Black currants add a wonderful tart element to this rustic betty, and because currants hold their shape when baked (much like a blueberry), they also make this dessert quite attractive to the eye. Be sure you do not confuse the plump black currants called for in this recipe, which look like ink-black gooseberries, with Zante currants, the small black raisins by the same name.

✛➤ BAKING TIME: 55 TO 65 MINUTES / SERVES 8 TO 12 ➤✛

1 tablespoon unsalted butter, at room temperature, for dish

6 large apples, peeled, cored, and sliced ¼ inch thick (3 pounds prepped)

1 cup (5 ounces) black currants, stemmed (see Kitchen Hint, page 46)

½ cup apple juice or apple cider

Zest and juice of 1 lemon

½ teaspoon fine sea salt

½ teaspoon ground cinnamon

¼ teaspoon freshly grated nutmeg

2 cups (5 ounces) crushed graham crackers or bread crumbs

½ cup (4 ounces) unsalted butter, melted

½ cup (3½ ounces) granulated sugar

Vanilla Bean Ice Cream (page 146), for serving

Position a rack in the lower third of the oven and preheat the oven to 350°F. Butter a 9-inch square baking dish.

Combine the apples and black currants in a bowl. Stir the apple juice, lemon zest and juice, salt, cinnamon, and nutmeg together in a liquid measuring cup, then stir into the fruit.

Stir the crumbs, melted butter, and sugar together, then sprinkle one-third of the crumbs over the bottom of the prepared pan. Spread half of the fruit over the crumbs in an even layer, top with another third of the crumbs, then top with the remaining fruit. Sprinkle the remaining crumbs over the fruit.

Cover with foil and bake in the lower third of the oven for 30 minutes, then remove the foil and bake for an additional 25 to 35 minutes, or until the topping is toasted and the filling is bubbling all over. Serve warm, topped with a scoop of Vanilla Bean Ice Cream.

Storage: This betty is best if eaten the day it is made. Any leftovers can be covered with a tea towel and eaten for breakfast or the next day's dessert. Reheat in a 300°F oven until warmed through.

huckleberry buckle with vanilla drizzle

This buckle is loaded with huckleberries. If you live in a region where huckleberries grow wild, it is fun to make a day of it and forage for the berries yourself. Otherwise, keep an eye out for huckleberries at your local farmers market. You could substitute wild blueberries if you cannot find huckleberries, but huckleberries are worth the search. Yogurt gives this buckle a zing. This buckle differs from others because it lacks a crumb topping and instead calls for a vanilla drizzle. This irresistible dessert is also perfect brunch fare.

BAKING TIME: 45 TO 55 MINUTES / SERVES 8 TO 12

1 tablespoon unsalted butter, at room temperature, for pan

BUCKLE

1¾ cups (8¾ ounces) all-purpose flour

2 teaspoons baking powder

½ teaspoon fine sea salt

½ cup (4 ounces) unsalted butter

¾ cup (5¼ ounces) granulated sugar

2 eggs

1 tablespoon pure vanilla extract

¾ cup (6 ounces) plain whole yogurt

2½ cups (11 ounces) huckleberries, fresh or frozen

2 tablespoons sliced almonds (optional)

VANILLA DRIZZLE

¾ cup (3¼ ounces) unsifted confectioners' sugar

1 tablespoon whole milk

½ teaspoon pure vanilla extract

Preheat the oven to 350°F. Butter a 9-inch round baking pan or 9-inch high-sided tart pan with a removable bottom.

To make the buckle, sift the flour, baking powder, and salt together in a bowl. Using a handheld mixer with beaters or a stand mixer with the paddle attachment, cream the butter and sugar together on medium-high speed for 3 to 5 minutes, until light and fluffy. Add the eggs one at a time, scraping down the sides of the bowl after each addition, then stir in the vanilla. Stir in the flour mixture in three additions alternating with the yogurt in two additions, beginning and ending with the dry ingredients and scraping down the sides of the bowl occasionally. Fold in 2 cups of the huckleberries; the batter will become very stiff if you are using frozen berries.

Spread the mixture into the prepared pan. Distribute the remaining ½ cup huckleberries over the cake and sprinkle with the almonds.

Bake for 45 to 55 minutes, or until lightly golden and a toothpick inserted in the middle comes out clean (although purple from the huckleberries). Cool for 20 minutes before removing from the pan and applying the vanilla drizzle.

To make the vanilla drizzle, sift the confectioners' sugar into a small bowl. Add the milk and vanilla and whisk until smooth. Drizzle over the buckle while it is still warm.

Storage: Wrapped in plastic wrap, the buckle will keep at room temperature for 2 to 3 days.

quince and apple brown butter tart

This beautiful tart would make a wonderful conclusion to a celebratory dinner. It takes some time to make, but it is worth every minute. Quince, a somewhat bumpy, golden fruit that has been described as the apple's poor relative, is making a comeback in the kitchen. Most varieties of quince are too hard, astringent, and sour to eat raw, but when cooked the flesh sweetens, turns a ruby red color, and has a fragrant aroma that more than makes up for its raw shortcomings. For this tart, the quince is poached; this is an additional step but oh so worth it to draw out this fruit's unique flavor. The quince and sliced apples are arranged in concentric circles, creating a visually stunning effect.

┼══ BAKING TIME: 35 TO 40 MINUTES / SERVES 8 TO 12 ══┼

1 recipe Short Dough (page 152), prebaked in a 10-inch fluted tart pan with removable bottom and cooled

POACHED QUINCE

3 cups water

1 cup (7 ounces) granulated sugar

½ lemon

3 quince, peeled, cored, and quartered (1½ pounds prepped)

To poach the quince, combine the water, sugar, and lemon half (peel and all) in a saucepan over medium heat and bring to a simmer. Adjust the heat as needed to maintain a simmer, then add the quince wedges. Put a clean tea towel over the fruit and weigh the towel down with a plate to keep the fruit submerged in the liquid. Poach for 10 to 40 minutes, depending on ripeness, until a paring knife inserted into the fruit meets no resistance. Try not to overcook the quince, lest they become mushy and fall apart. (Should this occur, just mash them up, spread the pulp on top of the pastry, and arrange the apples slices on top.) Cool the quince in the poaching liquid until ready to use; however, if you think the quince is getting overcooked, you should remove it from the liquid immediately. You can poach the quince up to 4 days before assembling the tart. Store the fruit in its poaching liquid in the refrigerator.

Preheat the oven to 375°F.

CUSTARD

6 tablespoons (3 ounces) unsalted butter

Seeds scraped from 1/2 vanilla bean (see Vanilla Beans, page 20)

2 eggs

1/4 teaspoon fine sea salt

1/2 cup (3 1/2 ounces) granulated sugar

1/3 cup (1 3/4 ounces) all-purpose flour

2 large apples, peeled, cored, and thinly sliced (1 pound prepped)

Crème fraîche (page 146) or Vanilla Bean Ice Cream (page 146), for serving

SEE HINT: "VANILLA BEANS" PAGE 20

To make the custard, melt the butter in a small saucepan or skillet over medium-high heat. Add the vanilla bean seeds and the pod to the saucepan. The butter will begin to foam and then subside. Continue to heat until the butter begins to brown and gives off a nutty aroma; it will smoke slightly. Remove from the heat and discard the vanilla bean pod. Beat the eggs with the salt and sugar in a small bowl, then slowly whisk the butter mixture into the eggs until evenly incorporated. Whisk in the flour.

Slice the poached quince quarters 1/4 to 1/2 inch thick and arrange them, alternating with the apple slices, in a circular pattern around the bottom of the tart shell, working your way from the outside to the inside. You may have more fruit than you need, which you can set aside to snack on while the tart cooks. Pour the custard evenly over the fruit. Do not worry about spreading it out; it will spread as it bakes.

Bake in the middle of the oven for 35 to 40 minutes, or until the center of the tart is firm. Cool for 20 minutes before serving with a small dollop of crème fraîche or a scoop of Vanilla Bean Ice Cream.

Storage: Covered with a tea towel, this tart will keep at room temperature for up to 3 days.

fig and mixed-color raspberry crumble

This elegant crumble is perfect for a fall harvest dinner. Its beauty comes from the fruit: The figs and raspberries are flash-broiled and therefore hold their sensuous shapes and vibrant colors. We suggest you use both golden and red raspberries, as the visual impact is stunning. The port-glazed figs add a depth of flavor to this otherwise simple dessert. The port reduction takes little time, and if you have made the crumble topping in advance, the rest of this recipe should take no more than 5 minutes.

BAKING TIME: 2 TO 5 MINUTES / SERVES 6

1 cup cold Vanilla Crumb (page 149)

2 tablespoons unsalted butter

¼ cup (1¾ ounces) granulated sugar

¼ cup tawny port

Pinch of fine sea salt

10 fresh figs, stemmed and quartered

½ dry pint (1 cup or 4½ ounces) red and golden raspberries

1 cup heavy cream, for serving

Preheat the broiler.

Melt the butter in a 9-inch broilerproof sauté pan. Stir in the sugar, port, and salt and bring to a simmer. Adjust the heat to maintain a simmer and cook, stirring occasionally, until the liquid is reduced by a third. Add the figs in a single layer, skin side down, and return to a simmer. The figs will begin to release their juices; once they do so, continue simmering until the liquid is once again reduced by a third.

Top with the raspberries and the cold Vanilla Crumb, then place the dessert under the broiler. Broil until the crumb turns golden and the raspberries have started to release their juices, 2 to 5 minutes. Be sure not to walk away from the oven; the timing is crucial and the dessert could burn in just a few seconds. As broilers perform differently, there is no set time for baking this dessert.

Spoon the dessert into individual bowls and serve with the cream in a pitcher on the side.

Storage: This crumble does not keep. It is meant to be served and consumed as soon as it is pulled from the oven.

pumpkin custard with cookie crumb crust

If you like pumpkin pie, you will love this custard. The flavors conjure up images of the fall harvest, as if to condense Thanksgiving into a ramekin. If you do not have ramekins or just feel creative, any other vessel may be used. We have even served this custard in teacups at a brunch. The cookie crumb crust takes on a dense texture as the crumb is saturated in the custard. If it strikes your fancy, you can use crisp gingersnaps instead of vanilla shortbread for the cookie crust.

+≈ **BAKING TIME: 50 TO 60 MINUTES / SERVES 8** ≈+

1¼ cups crushed Vanilla Bean Shortbread cookies (page 155; 6 to 8 cookies)

2 cups half-and-half

2 eggs

4 egg yolks

½ cup packed (3¾ ounces) brown sugar

½ cup (3½ ounces) granulated sugar

2 tablespoons Barbados (unsulfured) molasses

2 cups pureed cooked pumpkin, or 1 (15-ounce) can pumpkin puree

½ teaspoon fine sea salt

½ teaspoon ground cinnamon

½ teaspoon ground ginger

¼ teaspoon ground cloves

1 tablespoon pure vanilla extract

Chantilly cream (page 145), for garnish

Preheat the oven to 325°F. Divide the crushed cookies among eight 5-ounce ramekins.

In a small saucepan, bring the half-and-half to a light simmer over medium-low heat. Whisk the eggs and yolks together in a bowl, then whisk in both sugars and the molasses. Slowly pour the hot half-and-half into the egg mixture while whisking continuously. Stir the pumpkin, salt, cinnamon, ginger, cloves, and vanilla together in a large bowl. Slowly add the egg mixture, whisking just enough to combine ingredients; this will keep air bubbles to a minimum, which contributes to a creamier texture when baked.

Set a fine-mesh sieve over a 6-cup measuring cup or a bowl with a pour lip, then strain the custard into the measuring cup. Distribute the custard evenly among the ramekins, filling them almost to the top. Place a large roasting pan on the center rack of the oven, put the ramekins in the roasting pan, and carefully add enough hot water to the pan to come halfway up the sides of the ramekins.

Bake the custards for 50 to 60 minutes, or until puffed slightly on the edges and almost set when jiggled. Carefully remove the ramekins from the pan and place on a wire rack. Cool completely on the rack before covering lightly with plastic wrap and refrigerating for at least 5 hours and up to 2 days. Serve garnished with a small dollop of Chantilly cream.

Storage: The custard is best if eaten within 2 days, but any leftovers will keep in the refrigerator for up to 4 days.

KITCHEN HINT:

How to Make Pumpkin Puree

If you would rather make pumpkin puree than buy it in a can, find a small pie pumpkin (also called a sugar pumpkin), cut it in half, and scoop out the stringy guts and seeds. Preheat the oven to 350°F. Pour ¼ cup of water into a greased baking pan and lay the pumpkin cut side down in it. Bake for 40 to 50 minutes, until the pumpkin is very soft. Remove from the oven and flip the pumpkin cut side up to rest. Let cool, then scoop the meat into a fine-mesh sieve set over a bowl. Allow to strain overnight at room temperature (this allows the pumpkin meat to lose some of its water content). Stored in an airtight container in the refrigerator, the pumpkin puree will keep for up to 3 days.

pear cobbler with shingled hazelnut biscuits

This dessert is the quintessence of Pacific Northwest flavors. That said, people in any region of the country will love the combination of pears and hazelnuts. Overlapping the biscuits in a shingled pattern (like a roof) lends an attractive visual element. The high concentration of hazelnuts in the biscuit dough makes the cobbler less flaky—in a good way. You can use any pears for this recipe; if you use Bartlett pears, there is no need to peel them, as their thin skin will break down when baked.

⊹⊱ BAKING TIME: 55 TO 60 MINUTES / SERVES 8 TO 12 ⊰⊹

1 tablespoon unsalted butter, at room temperature, for dish

FRUIT FILLING

2/3 cup packed (5 ounces) medium brown sugar

3 tablespoons cornstarch

1/2 teaspoon fine sea salt

1/2 teaspoon ground cardamom

10 large firm but ripe pears, peeled, cored, and sliced or cubed (5 pounds prepped)

Juice of 1/2 lemon

Position a rack in the lower third of the oven and preheat the oven to 375°F. Butter a 9 by 13-inch baking dish.

To make the fruit filling, rub the brown sugar, cornstarch, salt, and cardamom together in a large bowl, then add the pears and lemon juice and toss until evenly coated. Spoon the fruit into the prepared pan, being sure to scrape the bowl well.

To make the biscuit, combine the flour, hazelnuts, sugar, baking powder, and salt in the bowl of a food processor and pulse until the nuts are finely chopped. Then add the butter and pulse until the butter is the size of peas, then transfer to a bowl. (Alternatively, you can chop the hazelnuts by hand and combine with the dry ingredients, then use your fingertips or a pastry blender to cut in the butter until the size of peas.) Pour in the 1/2 cup cream and stir just until the dry ingredients are moistened. The dough will be crumbly and appear very dry, but fear not; it will all come together.

BISCUIT

2 cups (10 ounces) all-purpose flour

1 cup (5 ounces) hazelnuts, toasted and skinned

3 tablespoons granulated sugar

1½ teaspoons baking powder

1 teaspoon fine sea salt

¾ cup (6 ounces) cold unsalted butter, cut into small cubes

½ cup plus 1 tablespoon cold heavy cream

Turn the dough out onto a lightly floured work surface and gently press the dough together to form a rectangle, then roll out to a rectangle measuring 8 by 15 inches (you may need some flour to prevent the rolling pin from sticking to the biscuit dough). Cut the rectangle in half lengthwise into 2 long skinny rectangles, each measuring 4 by 15 inches, then cut each rectangle crosswise into 5 slices, each about 3 inches in width. You should now have 10 biscuits, each measuring about 3 by 4 inches. Overlap the biscuits on top of the pear filling in a shingled pattern. Brush with the 1 tablespoon cream.

Cover the dish with foil and bake in the lower third of the oven for 20 minutes. Remove the foil and bake for an additional 35 minutes, or until the biscuits are golden and the filling is bubbling all over. Serve warm.

Storage: This cobbler is best if eaten the day it is made. Any leftovers can be covered with a tea towel to be finished for breakfast. Reheat in a 300°F oven until warmed through.

KITCHEN HINT:

Toasting Nuts

Toasting nuts not only brings out their flavor, it also makes it easier to remove the skin—especially from hazelnuts, one of our favorite ingredients. To toast nuts, place them in a heavy skillet over medium-high heat and shake the pan frequently to ensure that the nuts do not burn. Alternatively, you can place them in a 350°F oven. Once the nuts smell fragrant and begin to brown (about 10 minutes), remove them from the heat. They will continue to brown a bit as they cool. To remove hazelnut and almond skins, flip the nuts onto a clean kitchen towel and rub them inside the towel as if you were trying to dry them off. Some skins will cling to the nuts, but most will come off and stick to the towel. Do not worry about any skins remaining on the nuts.

upside-down pear chocolate cake

Chocolate and pears make an excellent combination. Here, bittersweet chocolate and sweet pears meld together to form the perfect balance. For this recipe, you can either take a rustic approach and toss the pears haphazardly into the pan or opt for a more elegant look by arranging the pears in concentric circles. Look for a good dark chocolate, which is not the same as unsweetened chocolate. Also, there are two kinds of unsweetened cocoa on the market; be sure to use unsweetened Dutch-processed cocoa, not natural cocoa. When combined with baking soda, natural cocoa can impart a bitter taste to baked goods and cause them to rise too much.

⇥⟩⟩⟩ BAKING TIME: 40 TO 45 MINUTES / SERVES 12 TO 15 ⟨⟨⟨⟨

1 tablespoon unsalted butter, at room temperature, for pan

FRUIT TOPPING

1 cup (7 ounces) granulated sugar

¼ cup water

3 firm but ripe pears, peeled, cored, and each cut into 12 slices (1 pound prepped)

SEE HINT: "MAKING CARAMEL" PAGE 71

Butter a 9-inch round baking pan.

To make the fruit topping, put the sugar and water in a heavy saucepan (one with a tight-fitting lid) and stir until the sugar dissolves. Bring the mixture to a boil over medium heat, then cover and cook for 2 minutes. (Covering in this way allows the steam to wash down the sides of pan, which will prevent any sugar crystals from forming.) Uncover the saucepan and continue to boil the sugar, gently and slowly swirling the pan as needed to cook the caramel evenly, until it becomes a dark amber color. Occasionally wash down the sides of the pan with a pastry brush dipped in cold water. Carefully pour the caramel into the prepared pan and allow it to harden. The pan will be very hot from the sugar, so take care in moving it if you need to. Fan the pear slices on top of the caramel in a circle around the perimeter, filling in the center with the remaining slices.

Preheat the oven to 350°F.

CONTINUED

upside-down pear chocolate cake, continued

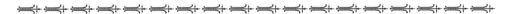

CAKE

¼ cup (2 ounces) unsalted butter

4 ounces dark chocolate, chopped

1 cup (5 ounces) all-purpose flour

⅓ cup (1 ounce) unsweetened
Dutch-processed cocoa powder

¾ teaspoon baking soda

½ teaspoon fine sea salt

¾ cup (5¼ ounces) granulated sugar

2 eggs

1 teaspoon pure vanilla extract

½ cup whole milk

Chantilly cream (page 145) or
Vanilla Bean Ice Cream (page 146),
for serving (optional)

To make the cake, place the butter and chocolate in a small saucepan over low heat and melt, stirring occasionally. Sift the flour, cocoa, baking soda, and salt together in a bowl. Transfer the melted chocolate to a mixing bowl or the bowl of a stand mixer and add the sugar. Using a handheld mixer with beaters or a stand mixer with the paddle attachment, beat on medium speed for about 3 minutes, until light and fluffy. Add the eggs one at time, scraping down the sides of the bowl after each addition. Stir in the vanilla. Stir in the flour mixture in three additions alternating with the milk in two additions, beginning and ending with the flour and scraping down the sides of the bowl occasionally.

Pour the batter into the prepared pan and bake in the middle of the oven for 40 to 45 minutes, or until the cake bounces back slightly when touched. Cool on a wire rack for 15 minutes, then invert the cake onto a plate, leaving the pan on top of the cake for 5 minutes before you remove it. Serve the cake warm, topped with a small dollop of Chantilly cream or a scoop of Vanilla Bean Ice Cream.

Storage: Wrapped in plastic wrap, the cake will keep at room temperature for up to 3 days.

caramel apple steamed pudding with ginger

The term "steamed pudding" sounds old-fashioned at best. And by "pudding," we mean cake. Steaming is a British method of cooking a cake in lieu of baking it in an oven. The effect is a very moist and dense yet fluffy cake. We spice up this old favorite by adding ginger—both candied and in dry form—to the steamed pudding. Some home bakers have a private collection of pudding molds and frequent antique stores in search of rare, vintage, or retro molds. While we applaud this enthusiasm, you do not need to be so avid to make this recipe. If you do not have a pudding mold handy, you can use a deep bowl covered tightly with foil.

BAKING TIME: 90 MINUTES / SERVES 8 TO 10

3 large apples

1 tablespoon unsalted butter

CARAMEL

¼ cup water

1 teaspoon freshly squeezed lemon juice

¾ cup (5¼ ounces) granulated sugar

SEE HINT: "MAKING CARAMEL" PAGE 71

Peel and core the apples. Slice 1½ apples ¼ inch thick. Melt the butter in a skillet over medium-high heat, then add the apple slices and cook without stirring until the apples are caramelized. Turn the slices over to brown the other side. Set aside to cool.

Grate the remaining 1½ apples. Set aside.

To make the caramel (see Making Caramel, page 71), put the water and lemon juice into a heavy saucepan. Add the sugar and stir until dissolved, then bring to a boil over medium heat without stirring. Occasionally wash down the sides of the pan with a pastry brush dipped in cold water, and gently swirl the pan to allow even heating. Stop cooking when the sugar turns pale amber. Pour the caramel into a pudding mold and, being very careful because the caramel is hot, swirl to coat the inside of the mold with caramel. The trick is to continuously tilt the mold, moving the liquid caramel around to prevent a pool of caramel from forming in the bottom of the mold. Continue tilting the mold until the caramel has cooled, then arrange the apple slices on top of the caramel.

CONTINUED

caramel apple steamed pudding with ginger, continued

PUDDING

1¾ cups (8¾ ounces) all-purpose flour

1 teaspoon baking soda

½ teaspoon fine sea salt

½ teaspoon ground cinnamon

½ teaspoon ground ginger

½ cup (2 ounces) finely chopped candied ginger

½ cup (4 ounces) unsalted butter, at room temperature

⅔ cup (4½ ounces) granulated sugar

¼ cup unsulfured molasses

2 eggs

½ cup buttermilk

Vanilla Sauce (page 149) made with apple brandy (preferably Calvados), for serving

To make the pudding, whisk the flour, baking soda, salt, cinnamon, and ground ginger together in a bowl, then stir in the candied ginger. Set a kettle of water on to boil.

Using a handheld mixer with beaters or a stand mixer with the paddle attachment, cream the butter, sugar and molasses together on medium-high speed for 3 to 5 minutes, until light and fluffy. Add the eggs one at a time, scraping down the sides of the bowl after each addition. Stir in the flour mixture in three additions alternating with the buttermilk in two additions, beginning and ending with the flour mixture and scraping down the sides of the bowl occasionally. Fold in the grated apples.

Spoon the batter into the mold, taking care not to disturb the apples, then gently tap the mold on a flat surface a few times to break up any air bubbles. Cover the mold tightly with a lid or heavy-duty aluminum foil, then set it in a saucepan large enough to allow at least 1 inch of space between the mold and the edge of the saucepan. Add enough boiling water to come halfway up the sides of the mold. Put the saucepan over medium-high heat and return to a boil, then lower the heat to maintain a gentle simmer, cover tightly, and cook for 90 minutes, checking the water level occasionally and adding more hot water if necessary. The pudding is done when the center springs back when lightly touched or when a wooden skewer inserted in the center comes out clean. Transfer the mold to a cooling rack, placing the mold upside down so the lid is on the bottom. Allow to cool for 15 minutes before removing the mold. You might need to rearrange the apples if some stick to the pan. Slice and serve while still warm, with brandy-spiked Vanilla Sauce on the side.

Storage: Wrapped in plastic wrap, the pudding will keep at room temperature for up to 5 days. It is best served warm; to reheat, cover the pudding with foil and heat in a 300°F oven until warmed through.

fig and honey cream galette

Sometimes when you bite into fresh figs, they drip as if they were already coated in honey; it is no wonder that these two flavors go so well together. Here, the honey pastry cream adds a sumptuous touch to this delicious dessert. For this recipe, select a flavorful honey that you enjoy. We prefer a strong honey with a pronounced flavor, such as clover honey or blackberry honey. Look for a local honey at the farmers market or a natural food store.

BAKING TIME: 50 TO 60 MINUTES / SERVES 8 TO 10

1 recipe Galette Dough (page 153)

PASTRY CREAM

Seeds scaped from ½ vanilla bean
(see Vanilla Beans, page 20)

¾ cup half-and-half

2 egg yolks

¼ cup honey

2 tablespoons granulated sugar

¼ teaspoon fine sea salt

1½ tablespoons cornstarch

2 tablespoons unsalted butter

8 to 10 large figs, stemmed and quartered

2 tablespoons granulated sugar

Crème fraîche (page 146),
for serving (optional)

SEE HINT: "VANILLA BEANS" PAGE 20

To make the pastry cream, put the vanilla bean seeds into a saucepan. Add the half-and-half and vanilla bean pod and cook over medium heat until hot, but not boiling. Separately, whisk the egg yolks, honey, sugar, and salt together in a bowl and continue whisking until slightly thickened and lighter in color. Add the cornstarch and whisk until combined. Slowly pour half of the hot liquid into the yolk mixture, stirring constantly until well blended. Pour the yolk mixture back into the saucepan and cook over medium heat, whisking constantly, until the mixture begins to thicken and bubble. Strain the mixture through a fine-mesh sieve, then whisk in the butter. Discard the vanilla bean pod. Stir occasionally until cool.

Line a baking sheet with parchment paper or grease it generously with cooking spray. Roll the dough into a 13- to 14-inch circle, then transfer to the prepared baking sheet. It should overhang the sheet a bit.

CONTINUED

Spread the cooled pastry cream over the dough, leaving a 2-inch border around the edge. Arrange the fig quarters in a circular pattern, skin side down and stem end facing into the center, again leaving a 2-inch border around the edge. Sprinkle the sugar over the figs. Fold the outer edge of the dough over the outermost figs, pleating the dough as necessary. Put the galette in the refrigerator for 1 hour to chill and relax the dough.

Position an oven rack in the lower third of the oven and preheat the oven to 375°F.

Bake the galette in the bottom third of the oven for 50 to 60 minutes. Cool for 30 minutes before serving, topped with a dollop of crème fraîche.

Storage: Covered with a tea towel, this galette will keep at room temperature for up to 2 days.

winter ⊶⊷⊶⊷⊶⊷⊶⊷⊶⊷

In winter, the days are shorter, the nights are longer, and friends and family gather to celebrate the holidays. What better time to enjoy a homemade fruit dessert! This is the season when people who usually do not attempt a dessert from scratch will try their hand at an apple pie, and when people who usually swear off sweets cannot resist a second helping. As families come together at the table, dessert becomes an excuse to linger and exchange stories. Do not be intimidated by cooking for a crowd; try the Caramelized Pear Bread Pudding (page 136), which is easy to make ahead for a large dinner party and will get rave reviews.

I always look forward to winter for its quiet bounty of flavor. This season, when fresh fruit is not available in great variety, presents the perfect opportunity to introduce dried fruit into your baking and cooking. From apricots to Zante currants, dried fruit offers concentrated sugar, color, and texture and intensifies the flavor of any compote or fruit pie.

This is also the season I reach—uncharacteristically, for those who know my penchant for local food—for citrus. The selection of citrus expands dramatically in winter. In addition to the standard choices of lemons, oranges, and grapefruits, many markets now sell hybrid varieties like tangelos (a cross between a grapefruit and a tangerine) and interesting cultivars, like the Cara Cara orange, a sweet orange with rosy pink flesh. When making the Olive Oil Citrus Cake (page 132), experiment with the unique flavors of blood oranges, named for the dark red color of their flesh, or Meyer lemons, a lemon with a slightly sweet, floral flavor. The clean, fresh taste of citrus livens up the winter months and reminds us that certain fruits thrive in what is considered the off-season.

These cold, crisp days also invite the bright taste of cranberries. The scarlet fruit's refreshing tart quality is often masked if you cook it with too much sugar. The result is a dull, cloying compote that may be fine on mashed potatoes, but leaves something to be desired as the focal point of a fruit dessert. I prefer to show off the berry's tangy bite by adding orange zest, fresh orange juice, and fresh ginger. Our cranberry dessert recipes call for buttermilk or sour cream to balance the cranberry's mouth-puckering tang. Try the Cranberry Buckle (page 118) if you want a sassy scarlet treat.

In summer, I make jam; in winter, I put up Pear Sauce (page 115). I suppose that I could make applesauce instead, but there is something quintessentially Oregon about using pears. I add spices to the pears and cook them slowly over low heat, and our home becomes redolent with the aromas of cinnamon or cardamom as the fruit simmers and the natural juices gradually reduce over the heat. Hours later, food mill in hand, I finish the fruit into sauce and pour it into glass jars, capturing winter in our pantry.

In Portland, we have a year-round farmers market where growers continue to sell their produce throughout the winter. In other regions, most folks return to the grocery store to buy fruit in winter, where they pick from the produce that is on the shelves. No matter what your source, it is helpful to have an idea of how to recognize ripe fruit in winter. Here are some tips on what to look for when selecting winter fruit:

APPLES

Apples should be bright and well-colored, with a smooth, shiny skin. Avoid any that are bruised or soft and choose firm ones instead. Aroma may also indicate ripeness and good flavor, although, unfortunately, apples are often picked early to avoid storage loss and shipping damage, in which case they may have no aroma at all. There are many varieties of apples to choose from, and you should not hesitate to ask for a sample if you are in doubt about which to buy. We have made some suggestions in our recipes for certain varieties we like, but do not feel restricted to our preferences if you find an intriguing variety at your farmers market. That said, certain apple varieties really do yield better results. Fresh varieties that often appear in winter markets and are used for baking include Fuji, Arkansas Black, Granny Smith, and Newton Pippin. You will also be able to find good keepers that have been stored after their earlier harvest, including varieties such as Stayman Winesap, Belle de Boskoop, Cortland, Melrose, and Jonathan. For winter applesauce, Cortland, Fuji, and Pink Lady apples are all good picks. For baked apples, seek out Macoun, Liberty, or Northern Spy apples. Apples store well in cold temperatures and may get mealy if left at room temperature for too long, so keep them in the refrigerator and use them within one week.

Apples have a natural light wax, sometimes called bloom, that seals and protects the apple and helps retain its water content. In the later months of the year, some growers apply a natural carnauba wax covering as a sealant to further protect the apple from drying out during storage. It can be removed by scrubbing the apple with a brush under lukewarm water. The apple's skin is durable and makes an excellent shell when baking whole apples. For other desserts, keep in mind that the texture of the apple skin will not break down much during baking. Also, the skin's color may affect the appearance of the dessert, especially if the skin is very dark red, such as Arkansas Black apples. Peeling the apple allows the fruit to break down and bake into the batter or topping of a recipe. When in doubt, peel the apple.

CITRUS

Contrary to what you would think, color is not a very good indicator of ripe citrus. Look instead for plump fruit with fine pores and smooth skin (a sign of thin skin, which is preferable to fruit with thick white pith). The skin should be tight and free of any bruises or brown spots. Fruit that is heavy for its size is preferable, as this indicates the fruit is full of juice. At room temperature, citrus will last for several days. Citrus is best stored in the refrigerator, where it will last longer.

CRANBERRIES

If you have the pleasure of buying fresh cranberries, look for berries that are shiny, not shriveled, and deep red in color. They should be hard and bounce when dropped (ask your grocer before conducting this test!). Soft or crushed cranberries do not have the same flavor, and you should avoid them. In the Pacific Northwest, we grow the common or northern cranberry; in the eastern United States and Canada, it is the large or American cranberry that finds its way to farmers markets. If you live in the northeastern United States, Michigan, or the coastal areas of the Pacific Northwest, where cranberry growers sell fruit at farmers markets, you can purchase a bulk amount and freeze any cranberries you do not use right away. Fresh cranberries will last for up to two weeks in the refrigerator.

PEARS

In winter, you may not be able to find any Bartlett pears at the market (they ripen early in the fall), but you should be able to find Comice pears if you want a pear that is tender and will bake quickly. Boscs and Anjous are naturally firmer and will take longer to break down when baked. Keep your eye out for Concorde pears, a Bosc-Comice cross that has the sweetness of a Comice and the hint of vanilla characteristic of a Bosc. Feel free to buy pears that are not yet ripe and allow them to sit at room temperature to achieve their characteristic sweetness. Look for pears that are bright and fresh (the color varies according to the variety, and only Bartletts change color noticeably as they ripen), and avoid any with bruises or soft spots. Check your pears daily to see if they are ripe by gently pressing near the stem. If the pear gives to gentle pressure, it is probably sweet and juicy on the inside and ready to use for baking. Pears do not keep long once they are ripe, but you can prolong their shelf life for a day or two by placing them in the refrigerator. Pear sauce is an ideal way to use very ripe fruit.

pear sauce

Bartlett, Comice, or Anjou pears all work well for this recipe because they have a high water content that will result in a sauce of thinner consistency. Bosc pears, on the other hand, will produce a thicker, chunkier sauce. You can also use apples instead of pears, in which case Gravenstein, McIntosh, or Cortland are the best choices. Use a heavy pot so the sauce does not burn on the bottom as it cooks down.

 **SERVES 6**

2½ cups apple cider or pear cider

2 tablespoons granulated sugar

3 whole cloves

2 whole star anise

1 cinnamon stick

¼ teaspoon cardamom

4 large pears, peeled, cored, and chopped (2 pounds prepped)

½ teaspoon pure vanilla extract

Juice of 1 lemon or orange

Combine the cider, sugar, cloves, star anise, cinnamon and cardamom in a large, heavy saucepan over high heat and bring to a boil. Lower the heat and simmer, stirring occasionally, for about 20 minutes, until reduced by half. Strain the cider and discard the spices.

Return the liquid to the pan, add the pears, cover, and simmer for 15 to 20 minutes, until the pears are tender. Remove from the heat and stir in the vanilla. Taste for sweetness and add either the lemon or orange juice (whichever you have on hand). Using a food mill with the medium sieve, mill the pears into a bowl and cool.

Storage: Stored in the refrigerator in a covered container, Pear Sauce will keep for at least 5 days.

pear sauce bundt cake
with pear brandy butter glaze

When my grandmother Virginia Richardson retired from New Jersey to Florida, far away from the local pears and apples of the Northeast, she passed her old food mill on to my mother, who in turn passed it on to me. In time, I purchased a new food mill, thinking that Grandma Richardson's was ready for retirement. The new mill has never matched up to the older one—too many bells and whistles for this New England girl! I now honor both my grandmother and her well-crafted food mill every time I have ripe pears ready to become sauce. Thick homemade sauce works best for this moist cake, but store-bought sauce works fine, too, in a pinch. Either hazelnuts or almonds are a great substitute for the walnuts, or you can omit the nuts altogether. Make the glaze right after you put the cake in the oven so it has time to cool before you pour it on the cake. —*Julie*

BAKING TIME: 50 TO 55 MINUTES / SERVES 12 TO 15

1 tablespoon unsalted butter, at room temperature, for pan

CAKE

2¾ cups (13¾ ounces) all-purpose flour

5 tablespoons (¾ ounce) Dutch-processed cocoa powder

2½ teaspoons baking soda

¾ teaspoon fine sea salt

1½ teaspoons freshly grated nutmeg

1½ teaspoons ground cinnamon

14 tablespoons (7 ounces) unsalted butter

2 cups (14 ounces) granulated sugar

3 eggs

Preheat the oven to 375°F. Butter a 10- to 12-cup Bundt pan.

To make the cake, sift the flour, cocoa, baking soda, salt, nutmeg, and cinnamon together in a bowl. Using a handheld mixer with beaters or a stand mixer with the paddle attachment, cream the butter and sugar together on medium-high speed for 3 to 5 minutes, until light and fluffy. Add the eggs one at a time, scraping down the sides of the bowl after each addition. Stir in the flour mixture in three additions alternating with the Pear Sauce in two additions, beginning and ending with the flour mixture and scraping down the sides of the bowl occasionally. Finely chop the walnuts and add them with the last addition of the flour mixture.

Pour the mixture into the prepared pan and bake for 50 to 55 minutes, or until a skewer inserted in the middle comes out moist but not wet and the cake is firm. Cool on a wire rack for 20 minutes before inverting onto the cooling rack, then cool for an additional 20 minutes before glazing.

2 cups Pear Sauce (page 115)

1 cup (4 ounces) raw walnuts

BRANDY GLAZE

½ cup packed (3¾ ounces) brown sugar

⅓ cup heavy cream

¼ cup (2 ounces) unsalted butter

Pinch of fine sea salt

2 tablespoons pear brandy

Place parchment paper or a baking sheet beneath the rack to collect the drips when you glaze the cake.

To make the brandy glaze, combine the sugar, cream, butter, and salt in a small saucepan over medium-high heat and bring to a low boil. Gently boil the glaze for 5 minutes, adjusting the heat as needed and stirring occasionally. Remove from the heat and stir in the brandy.

Allow the sauce to cool for 1 hour, stirring occasionally. The sauce will thicken but still be pourable. Spread the glaze over the cake while the cake is still slightly warm.

Storage: This is a great keeper! Wrapped in plastic wrap, the cake will stay moist at room temperature for up to 4 days.

cranberry buckle with vanilla crumb

When the cranberries in this buckle bake, they split open just enough to absorb the cake batter while retaining a firm outer shell and a slightly tart bite. Half are folded into the batter and half are distributed on top with the Vanilla Crumb, creating a red-jeweled delight. This recipe is great for a holiday breakfast or brunch.

BAKING TIME: 45 TO 50 MINUTES / SERVES 8 TO 12

1 tablespoon unsalted butter, at room temperature, for pan

1 cup Vanilla Crumb (page 149)

1¾ cups (8¾ ounces) all-purpose flour

2 teaspoons baking powder

½ teaspoon fine sea salt

½ cup (4 ounces) unsalted butter

¾ cup (5¼ ounces) granulated sugar

Zest of 1 orange (see Zesting Citrus, page 134)

2 eggs

1 tablespoon pure vanilla extract

½ cup (5 ounces) sour cream

2 cups (8 ounces) cranberries, fresh or frozen

Preheat the oven to 350°F. Butter a 9-inch square baking pan.

Sift the flour, baking powder, and salt together in a bowl. Using a handheld mixer with beaters or a stand mixer with the paddle attachment, cream the butter, sugar, and orange zest together on medium-high speed for 3 to 5 minutes, until light and fluffy. Add the eggs one at a time, scraping down the sides of the bowl after each addition, then stir in the vanilla. Stir in the flour mixture in three additions alternating with the sour cream in two additions, beginning and ending with the flour mixture and scraping down the sides of the bowl occasionally. Fold in 1 cup of the cranberries.

Spread the mixture into the prepared pan. Distribute the remaining 1 cup cranberries over the cake and sprinkle the crumb topping over the cranberries.

Bake for 45 to 50 minutes, or until lightly golden and firm on top.

Storage: Wrapped in plastic wrap, this cake will keep at room temperature for 2 to 3 days.

SEE HINT: "ZESTING CITRUS" PAGE 134

cranberry upside-down almond cake

Baker & Spice uses a wonderful natural almond paste from Mandelin, a California company that grows the almonds it uses to make paste (see the Sources section). Mandelin's natural almond paste has a lower ratio of sugar to almonds, giving it a more pronounced almond flavor. If you cannot find a natural paste, any almond paste will do—but not marzipan, which is a sweeter product with as much as three parts sugar to one part almonds, whereas almond paste usually has equal amounts of sugar and almonds. Look in the baking aisle of any well-stocked grocery store to find almond paste. The flavor combination of cranberries and almonds is a knockout, heightened here by almonds in two forms: almond paste in the batter and sliced almonds in the topping. This is a great dessert worthy of any holiday table.

BAKING TIME: 60 TO 65 MINUTES / SERVES 10 TO 12

1 tablespoon unsalted butter, at room temperature, for pan

FRUIT TOPPING

3 tablespoons unsalted butter, melted

½ cup packed (3¾ ounces) brown sugar

¼ cup (¾ ounce) sliced almonds

3 cups (12 ounces) cranberries, fresh or frozen

CAKE

1¾ cups (8¾ ounces) all-purpose flour

1½ teaspoons baking powder

½ teaspoon fine sea salt

14 tablespoons (7 ounces) unsalted butter

Preheat the oven to 350°F. Butter a 9-inch round baking pan.

To make the fruit topping, melt the butter in a small saucepan, then remove from the heat and stir in the brown sugar. Pour the mixture into the prepared pan and spread it in an even layer. Sprinkle the almonds over the sugar mixture, then evenly distribute the cranberries in the pan.

To make the cake, sift the flour, baking powder, and salt together in a bowl. Using a handheld mixer with beaters or a stand mixer with the paddle attachment, cream the butter, almond paste, and sugar together on medium-high speed for 3 to 5 minutes, until light and fluffy. Add the eggs one at a time, scraping down the sides of the bowl after each addition, then stir in the vanilla. Stir in the flour mixture in three additions alternating with the buttermilk in two additions, beginning and ending with the flour mixture and scraping down the sides of the bowl occasionally. Gently spread the batter over the cranberries in an even layer.

Bake for 60 to 65 minutes. Cool for 20 minutes.

⅓ cup packed (4 ounces) almond paste

¾ cup (5¼ ounces) granulated sugar

3 eggs

1 tablespoon pure vanilla extract

½ cup buttermilk

Crème fraiche (page 146) or Chantilly cream (page 145), for serving (optional)

To flip the cake out of its pan, first run a knife around the edges, then place a flat plate or serving platter facedown over the top of the cake and quickly invert the cake onto the platter in one fell swoop. Serve with a dollop of crème fraiche or Chantilly cream.

Storage: Wrapped in plastic wrap, this cake will keep at room temperature for 2 to 3 days.

KITCHEN HINT:

Freezing Fruit

Although we are always in favor of using fresh fruit in season, frozen fruit can be used in many of the recipes in this book. Freezing fruit allows you to preserve it at the peak of its season, when it is most abundant and flavorful, and it is easy to do. In all cases, only freeze fruit when it is at the peak of freshness. Here are some tips for specific fruits.

- BERRIES AND CURRANTS: Just pop baskets of berries or currants into your freezer, without washing them first. Once the berries or currants are frozen, transfer them to a freezer bag.

- STONE FRUIT: Pit and slice the fruit, then lay the slices in a single layer on a baking sheet and pop the pan in the freezer. Once the fruit is frozen, transfer the slices to a freezer bag.

- RHUBARB: Wash and dry the rhubarb stalks, cutting off the leaves and ends. Chop the rhubarb into 1- to 2-inch pieces and lay the pieces in a single layer on a baking sheet and pop the pan in the freezer. Once the rhubarb is frozen, transfer the pieces to a freezer bag.

apple cranberry oat crumble

Apples and cranberries complement one another and look beautiful on the plate—picture scarlet cranberries popping out from amber apple filling. This crumble has a high ratio of crumble to fruit and is a delicious dessert to serve at the end of Thanksgiving dinner. Just be sure you have some vanilla ice cream or Chantilly cream at the ready!

+ ══ BAKING TIME: 60 TO 70 MINUTES / SERVES 8 TO 12 ══ +

1 tablespoon unsalted butter, at room temperature, for dish

TOPPING

2 cups (7 ounces) rolled oats

1½ cups (7½ ounces) all-purpose flour

1⅓ cups packed (10 ounces) brown sugar

½ teaspoon fine sea salt

¾ cup (6 ounces) unsalted butter, melted

FRUIT FILLING

8 large apples, peeled, cored, and sliced ¼ inch thick (3½ pounds prepped)

2 cups (8 ounces) cranberries, fresh or frozen

1⅓ cups (9¼ ounces) granulated sugar

2 tablespoons cornstarch

2 teaspoons ground cinnamon

Vanilla Bean Ice Cream (page 146) or Chantilly cream (page 145), for serving (optional)

Preheat the oven to 375°F. Butter a 3-quart baking dish.

To make the topping, mix the oats, flour, brown sugar, and salt together in a bowl. Stir in the butter, then press the topping together with your hands to form small clumps. Put the topping in the freezer while you assemble the filling.

To make the fruit filling, toss the apples, cranberries, sugar, cornstarch, and cinnamon together in a large bowl. Transfer the filling to the prepared pan and spread it out, pressing the fruit down into the corners.

Press the oat crumble evenly over the fruit, then bake for 60 to 70 minutes, or until the crumble is lightly golden and the filling is bubbling up in the corners. Cool for 20 minutes or so to temper the heat before serving, then top with a scoop of Vanilla Bean Ice Cream or a small dollop of Chantilly cream.

Storage: This crumble is best if served the day it is made, but any leftovers can be wrapped in plastic wrap and kept at room temperature for 2 to 3 days. Reheat in a 300°F oven for 10 to 15 minutes, until warm.

apple custard pie with orange

For this recipe, select firm and slightly tangy apples with lower water content, such as Granny Smith, Braeburn, Green Sweet, or Pippin. Baking the apples without the custard first allows them to soften and settle into the crust. When the pie cools, the creamy, orange-scented custard layers with the crunchy apples, making each spoonful a textural surprise. Also, use orange oil, not orange extract, because orange oil adds a deeper flavor.

BAKING TIME: 55 MINUTES / SERVES 6 TO 8

¼ recipe (1 disk) All-Butter Pie Pastry (page 153), baked halfway and cooled

FRUIT FILLING

3 large apples, peeled, cored, and thinly sliced (1 pound prepped)

2 tablespoons granulated sugar

¼ cup freshly squeezed orange juice (about ½ orange)

CUSTARD

2 eggs

3 tablespoons granulated sugar

⅛ teaspoon fine sea salt

2 tablespoons orange zest (about 1 large orange)

¼ teaspoon ground cinnamon

¼ teaspoon freshly grated nutmeg

¼ teaspoon ground ginger

⅓ cup whole milk

⅓ cup heavy whipping cream

¼ teaspoon orange oil (optional)

2 tablespoons granulated sugar, for topping pie

Position a rack in the lower third of the oven and preheat the oven to 375°F.

To make the fruit filling, toss the apples with the sugar and orange juice, then transfer to the partially baked pie shell. Bake in the lower third of the oven for 25 minutes while you make the custard.

To make the custard, whisk the eggs, sugar, salt, and zest together in a bowl. Stir in the cinnamon, nutmeg, and ginger, then add the milk, cream, and orange oil and stir to combine.

Remove the pie from the oven, pour the custard over the apples, and sprinkle with the 2 tablespoons sugar. Return to the oven and bake for an additional 30 minutes, or until the custard puffs up on the sides and the apples begin to turn golden brown.

Storage: This pie is best if served the day it is made, but any leftovers can be wrapped in plastic wrap and kept in the refrigerator for 2 to 3 days. It is great for breakfast the next day!

SEE HINT: "ZESTING CITRUS" PAGE 134

Mimi's German apple cake

Growing up in rural Vermont meant that visiting friends was not always a stroll next door. I used to trek up a big hill to visit one grade school friend, but it was always well worth the trip for the camaraderie and for her German grandmother's tea cake. It was a traditional German butter cake with local McIntosh apples nestled in the batter and cinnamon sugar sprinkled on top. Mimi (my friend's grandmother) taught me that scoring the apples with a fork helps ensure they will be tender by the time the cake is baked to perfection. I have adapted the recipe by sprinkling turbinado sugar over the cake; I think it adds a nice texture. This recipe takes only fifteen minutes of prep time before it goes into the oven. —*Julie*

╬══ BAKING TIME: 40 MINUTES / SERVES 6 TO 10 ══╬

1 tablespoon unsalted butter, at room temperature, for pan

1 cup (5 ounces) all-purpose flour

1 teaspoon baking powder

¼ teaspoon fine sea salt

½ cup (4 ounces) unsalted butter

½ cup (3½ ounces) granulated sugar

Zest of 1 lemon

2 eggs

1 teaspoon pure vanilla extract

2 apples, peeled, cored, and each cut into 6 pieces

2 tablespoons turbinado sugar

SEE HINT: "ZESTING CITRUS" PAGE 134

Preheat the oven to 350°F. Butter a 9-inch round baking pan.

Sift the flour, baking powder, and salt together in a bowl. Using a handheld mixer with beaters or a stand mixer with the paddle attachment, cream the butter, sugar, and lemon zest on medium-high speed for 3 to 5 minutes, until light and fluffy. Add the eggs one at a time, scraping down the sides of the bowl after each addition, then stir in the vanilla. Add the flour mixture all at once and mix on low speed just until incorporated. Pour the batter into the prepared pan.

Score the peeled side of the apples with the tines of a fork and arrange the apples atop the batter around the perimeter, with 1 slice in the center. Sprinkle the turbinado sugar over the cake and bake for about 40 minutes, or until the cake is lightly golden and a toothpick inserted in the center comes out clean. Sometimes the batter around the apples looks slightly underdone, but not to worry; it is just the moisture from the apples.

Storage: Wrapped in plastic wrap, this cake will keep at room temperature for 2 to 3 days.

apple cobbler with cheddar cheese biscuits

When working as a teenager in my family's century-old Portland restaurant, Dan and Louis Oyster Bar, I remember thinking what an odd combination it was when a customer requested a slice of white cheddar cheese to accompany the apple pie. After I moved to New England years later, I finally began to understand why this combination is so popular. This recipe offers an innovative twist to the usual combination, folding the cheese into the biscuit dough baked on top of the apples. Braeburn, Cameo, or Jonagold are ideal apple varieties for this cobbler, and a Grafton white cheddar from Vermont would make a New Englander feel right at home. —*Cory*

⁓ BAKING TIME: 50 TO 60 MINUTES / SERVES 8 TO 10 ⁓

1 tablespoon unsalted butter, at room temperature, for dish

FRUIT FILLING

1 cup packed (7½ ounces) medium brown sugar

3 tablespoons cornstarch

½ teaspoon fine sea salt

1 teaspoon ground cinnamon

8 large apples, peeled, cored, and sliced ¼ inch thick (3½ pounds prepped)

Juice of 1 lemon

¼ cup (2 ounces) unsalted butter

Position a rack in the lower third of the oven and preheat the oven to 375°F. Butter a 3-quart baking dish.

To make the fruit filling, with your hands, rub the brown sugar, cornstarch, salt, and cinnamon together in a large bowl. Add the apples and toss to evenly coat. Gently stir in the lemon juice. Let the apples sit for 15 minutes to release some of their juices. Mix the filling one more time before scraping the contents into the prepared pan. Cut the butter into small cubes and scatter over the apples.

Cover the pan with foil and bake in the lower third of the oven for 20 minutes. This gives the apples a jump start on cooking while you make the biscuits.

BISCUIT

2 cups (10 ounces) all-purpose flour

2 tablespoons granulated sugar

2 teaspoons baking powder

1/2 teaspoon fine sea salt

2 cups (4 ounces) grated extra-sharp cheddar cheese

1 1/3 cups cold buttermilk, or more as needed

To make the biscuits, whisk the flour, 1 tablespoon of the sugar, the baking powder, and salt together in a bowl. Add the cheese and toss until evenly coated. Make a well in the center of the bowl and add the buttermilk. With a rubber spatula or fork, or by hand, stir just until the dry ingredients are moistened. The dough will be shaggy and moist. If the dough seems dry, add a bit more buttermilk, no more than 1 tablespoon at a time.

Take the baking pan out of the oven and remove the foil. In 1/4-cup portions, place the dough atop the fruit, distributing the biscuits evenly. (You should end up with about 9 biscuits.) Sprinkle the remaining 1 tablespoon sugar over the biscuits.

Return the cobbler to the oven (this time without the foil) and bake for an additional 30 to 40 minutes, or until the apples are tender, the juices are bubbling, and the biscuits are golden brown.

Storage: This dessert is best served the day it is made, but any leftovers can be wrapped in plastic wrap (or foil) and kept at room temperature for 2 to 3 days.

deep-dish winter fruit pie with walnut crumb

This deep-dish crumb-topped pie combines several winter fruits and confirms that the whole is greater than the sum of its parts. The pears become soft, the apples remain slightly firm, the figs add texture and sweetness, and the tart cranberries pop in your mouth, making this rustic pie a sensory treat. Be sure to plan ahead, as this recipe calls for chilling the dough for one hour, chilling it again after you roll it out (this reduces shrinkage of the crust during baking), and then baking the pie for over an hour. It is an hours-long process, off and on, but it is worth every minute. Served with a scoop of vanilla ice cream and a glass of apple or pear brandy (preferably from Clear Creek Distillery), it is the perfect final touch to a dinner party.

BAKING TIME: 60 TO 75 MINUTES / SERVES 8 TO 10

PIE PASTRY

1¾ cups (8¾ ounces) all-purpose flour

1 tablespoon granulated sugar

½ teaspoon fine sea salt

12 tablespoons (6 ounces) cold unsalted butter, cut into ½-inch cubes

3 tablespoons ice water

1 teaspoon freshly squeezed lemon juice

To make the pie pastry, put the flour, sugar, and salt in a bowl, stir to combine, then put the bowl in the freezer for 10 minutes.

Add the butter to the flour mixture and toss to evenly coat. Cut the butter into the flour mixture using a pastry blender, a food processor, an electric mixer, or your hands, just until the mixture becomes coarse and crumbly and the butter is the size of peas. Stir the water and lemon juice together, then pour over the dry ingredients and stir just until the dry ingredients are moistened.

Dump the dough onto a well-floured work surface and press it into a 6-inch disk. Wrap in plastic wrap and refrigerate for at least 1 hour.

Roll the chilled dough into a 14-inch disk, then line a 9 or 10 by 3-inch springform pan with the rolled-out dough. Patch any holes and trim off any dough that hangs over the edges of the pan. Chill for an additional 30 minutes while you prepare the crumb topping and the fruit filling.

CONTINUED

WALNUT CRUMB TOPPING

¾ cup (3¾ ounces) all-purpose flour

¾ cup packed (5¾ ounces) brown sugar

¾ cup (3 ounces) raw walnuts, coarsely chopped

1½ teaspoons ground cinnamon

¼ teaspoon fine sea salt

6 tablespoons (3 ounces) unsalted butter, melted

FRUIT FILLING

1 cup (5½ ounces) dried figs

4 small apples, peeled, cored, and sliced ½ inch thick (12 ounces prepped)

4 pears, peeled, cored, and sliced ½ inch thick (1¼ pounds prepped)

1 cup (4 ounces) cranberries, fresh or frozen

½ cup (3½ ounces) granulated sugar

2 tablespoons cornstarch

To make the walnut crumb topping, mix the flour, brown sugar, walnuts, cinnamon, and salt together in a bowl. Stir in the butter, then work it in with your hands until the texture of crumbs. Put the topping in the refrigerator while you make the fruit filling.

Position a rack in the lower third of the oven and preheat the oven to 375°F.

To make the fruit filling, remove the stem from each fig, then boil the figs in 1 cup of water for 5 minutes. Drain and set aside until cool enough to handle.

Slice each fig into 4 to 5 pieces, put them in a large bowl, and add the apples, pears, and cranberries. Separately, rub the sugar and cornstarch together, then add to the fruit and gently toss until evenly coated.

Transfer the filling to the pie shell and top with the walnut crumb. Bake in the lower third of the oven for 60 to 75 minutes, or until the crumb is golden, the fruit juices are bubbling thickly around the edges, and the fruit is tender when pierced with a wooden skewer. If the crumb is getting too dark, cover it with foil.

Storage: Covered with a tea towel, the pie will keep at room temperature for up to 3 days. Spooned into a bowl and drizzled with chilled cream, it makes a wonderful breakfast.

stewed fruit and chantilly cream
with vanilla bean shortbread

I like to use unfiltered apple cider for stewing fresh or dried fruit whenever I make compote. When reduced, apple cider provides a natural sugar base that blends well with other fruits. A medley of different-sized dried fruits works best for this recipe, so I throw in chunks of apricots, prunes, plums, and pears, as well as dried sour cherries and golden raisins. You could also use dried peaches, apples, or Zante currants, which have an intense, sweet flavor. (They are small dried seedless grapes that look like tiny dark raisins; do not confuse them with currants.) Feel free to improvise on the spices. Vanilla Bean Shortbread makes a perfect accompaniment, but you might also like to try a few thin slices of fresh apple or pear atop the cream for contrast. —*Cory*

 **SERVES 6**

Vanilla Bean Shortbread (page 155), for serving

STEWED FRUIT

Seeds scraped from 1 vanilla bean (see Kitchen Hint, page 20)

1 cup red wine (Zinfandel, Merlot, or Syrah)

1½ cups unfiltered apple cider

2 tablespoons honey

1 cinnamon stick

2 whole star anise

2 whole cloves

2½ cups dried fruit medley of your choice, chopped

4 cups (2 recipes) Chantilly cream (page 145), for serving

To make the stewed fruit, put the vanilla bean seeds into a saucepan. Add the vanilla bean pod, wine, apple cider, honey, cinnamon, anise, and cloves and cook over medium-high heat until simmering. Lower the heat to maintain a simmer and continue cooking, stirring occasionally, until the liquid is reduced by one-third. Add the dried fruit and simmer, stirring occasionally, for about 20 minutes, until the dried fruit has absorbed most of the liquid, leaving a small amount that resembles syrup. The syrup should become thick and glaze the fruit. Remove from the heat and cool to room temperature. The whole spices will bloom as the liquid cools, so remove them early if you do not want their flavors to dominate. You can stew the fruit up to 2 days in advance. Cover and store in the refrigerator. To serve, spoon the fruit (preferably warm) into serving dishes, top with a generous dollop of Chantilly Cream, and serve with a shortbread cookie alongside.

Storage: Stored in an airtight container in the refrigerator, stewed fruit will keep for up to 1 week. In contrast, the Chantilly cream should be eaten up!

olive oil citrus cake

Baker & Spice strives to use local products but bends the rules when it comes to citrus fruit. The bakery features citrus-flavored desserts in the winter months when markets teem with a wide array of citrus. Fruits such as Meyer lemons, Indian River grapefruits, Minneola tangelos, and Cara Cara oranges all impart unique citrus flavors to baking. Try to find attractive fruits to yield the best zest for this recipe. The citrus flavors are further enhanced by the addition of lemon oil, which adds a deeper, complex flavor. This cake is moist and easy; if you want to skip the glaze, just dust the cake with confectioners' sugar (sift it onto the cake just before serving for best results).

When using olive oil for baking, choose a fruity olive oil with a medium density and lasting thickness on the tongue. You want to avoid strong extra-virgin oil with a spicy bite or a second or third pressing pomace oil, which will contribute neither color nor flavor to the cake batter. Taste a small amount of olive oil with a little citrus zest or juice before pouring it into the batter. If you like how the flavors blend, pour away!

✢ BAKING TIME: 25 TO 30 MINUTES / SERVES 8 TO 10 ✢

CAKE

1¼ cups unsifted (5 ounces) cake flour (you will sift it later)

1 teaspoon baking powder

¼ teaspoon fine sea salt

3 eggs, at room temperature

1 tablespoon plus ¾ cup (5¼ ounces) granulated sugar

Zest of 1 grapefruit

Zest of 1 orange

Zest of 1 lemon

1½ teaspoons pure vanilla extract

¼ teaspoon lemon oil (optional)

1 cup extra-virgin olive oil

Preheat the oven to 350°F. Using a paper towel, coat a 9-inch by 2-inch round baking pan with olive oil, then sprinkle it with about 1 tablespoon of granulated sugar.

To make the cake, sift the flour, baking powder, and salt together *twice*. Using a handheld mixer or stand mixer with the whisk attachment, beat the eggs, sugar, and zests on high speed for 5 minutes, until the eggs are thickened and lighter in color. Add the vanilla and lemon oil. Turn the mixer down to medium-low speed and drizzle the olive oil into the batter, pouring slowly along the edge of the bowl. Add the flour and mix on low speed until just incorporated. Pour the batter into the prepared pan.

Bake for 25 to 30 minutes, or until the cake is golden and has domed slightly in the center. Cool to room temperature.

CONTINUED

olive oil citrus cake, continued

GLAZE

¾ cup (3¼ ounces)
confectioners' sugar

2 tablespoons freshly squeezed
grapefruit juice

To make the glaze, sift the confectioners' sugar into a small bowl. Add the grapefruit juice and whisk to combine. Pour the glaze over the cooled cake.

Storage: Wrapped in plastic wrap, this cake will keep at room temperature for 2 to 3 days.

KITCHEN HINT:

Zesting Citrus

Zest is the very outermost skin of citrus fruit. It imparts a fragrant citrus flavor that is not bitter (the bitter taste comes from the pith, the white flesh between the outer skin of the fruit and the segments). Be sure to wash citrus before zesting it, to get rid of any wax coating or impurities picked up between the orchard and your kitchen. We prefer organic citrus for zesting. One medium lemon will generally yield 1 tablespoon of zest. Although you can try to cut the outermost skin from the citrus using a sharp knife or a potato peeler, you would still need to mince it to create zest. It is easier to use a zester (a gadget that looks like a peeler with tiny cutting holes that create thin strips of zest) or a microplane grater (which will produce grated zest—best for our recipes). A basic cheese grater will also work if you use the smallest holes. If you will be using both the zest and the juice of a citrus fruit, zest the fruit first, as it is so much easier to zest citrus when the fruit is whole.

lemon sponge tart

My grandmother Betty Merz is a tried-and-true Pennsylvanian. She grew up and lived for eighty years in Philadelphia County, which lies east of the Amish county of Lancaster, where this recipe originated. When my grandmother retired from baking and moved to Oregon, she passed her collection of favorite recipes on to me. Among them, I found five slightly different versions of this lemon sponge pie recipe, which goes to show how popular it was. I have updated it by changing the pie crust to a prebaked tart shell for crunchiness, adding additional lemon juice, and decreasing the sugar. It is a wonderful cross between a lemon bar and a lemon meringue pie, but better than both. Thanks, Grams, for the inspiration and the recipes! —*Julie*

BAKING TIME: 28 TO 33 MINUTES / SERVES 8 TO 12

1 recipe Short Dough (page 152), baked in a 10-inch fluted tart pan with a removable bottom and cooled

2 tablespoons unsalted butter, at room temperature

¾ cup (5¼ ounces) granulated sugar

Zest of 2 lemons

2 eggs, separated

Juice of 2 lemons

2½ tablespoons all-purpose flour

¾ cup whole milk

½ teaspoon fine sea salt

SEE HINT: "WHIPPING EGG WHITES" PAGE 157

Preheat the oven to 425°F.

Using a handheld mixer with beaters or a stand mixer with the paddle attachment, beat the butter, sugar, and lemon zest at medium speed until well combined. Add the egg yolks one at a time, scraping down the sides of the bowl after each addition and mixing until the batter is creamy. Stir in the lemon juice, then stir in the flour until evenly incorporated. Add the milk and mix on low speed until combined. The mixture will be very thin.

In a clean metal bowl, whisk the egg whites and salt by hand until soft peaks form. Gently fold the egg whites into the lemon mixture until all of the ingredients are evenly incorporated. Pour into the prebaked tart shell.

Put the tart on a baking sheet to catch any drips and bake for 8 minutes, then turn the oven down to 325°F and bake for an additional 20 to 25 minutes, or until the filling is golden and firm to the touch. Cool to room temperature before serving.

Storage: Wrapped in plastic wrap, the tart will keep at room temperature for up to 3 days. The crust will get a bit soggy over time, but it will still taste great.

caramelized pear bread pudding

The trio of aromatic caramelized pears, toasty sweet bread, and vanilla custard makes this bread pudding a rich yet simple dessert. It tastes great on its own or adorned with Vanilla Sauce spiked with pear brandy. Use ripe but firm pears (Bartletts are a particularly good variety), as they need to stand up to high heat during caramelizing. Either challah or brioche is great for this recipe (save the scraps from old loaves in your freezer until you have enough for the recipe), but you could substitute a day-old baguette or two instead; just use the larger amount of sugar and an extra egg. If time allows, soak the bread in the custard overnight in the refrigerator before baking. And no, $\frac{1}{4}$ cup of vanilla is not a typo! We use this much because vanilla is a prominent flavor in this bread pudding.

✦✦ BAKING TIME: 40 TO 45 MINUTES / SERVES 8 TO 12 ✦✦

1 tablespoon unsalted butter, at room temperature, for dish

PUDDING

5 or 6 eggs

$\frac{1}{3}$ to $\frac{1}{2}$ cup (2$\frac{1}{4}$ to 4 ounces) granulated sugar

$\frac{1}{4}$ cup pure vanilla extract

Pinch of fine sea salt

2 cups whole milk

1 cup heavy cream

1$\frac{1}{2}$ pounds stale bread, cut into 1-inch to 1$\frac{1}{2}$-inch cubes (about 10 cups)

Preheat the oven to 350°F. Butter a 3-quart baking dish.

To make the pudding, whisk the eggs, sugar, vanilla, and salt together in a bowl large enough to hold all of the pudding ingredients. Whisk in the milk and cream. Add the bread and push down on the bread to submerge it in the custard. At this point, ideally, you would cover the bowl and refrigerate it overnight, but you can also just continue with the recipe, occasionally stirring or pushing down on the bread to keep it covered with the custard.

FRUIT TOPPING

6 tablespoons (3 ounces) unsalted butter

¾ cup (5¼ ounces) granulated sugar

6 to 8 pears, peeled, cored, and quartered (2 pounds prepped)

Vanilla Sauce (page 149) made with pear brandy, for serving (optional)

To make the fruit topping, melt the butter over low heat in a skillet large enough to hold all of the pears in a single layer. Sprinkle the sugar evenly over the melted butter and lay the pears over the sugar. Turn the heat to high and let the pears cook undisturbed for 8 to 10 minutes. Once the juices and pears begin to caramelize, carefully shake the pan to distribute the heat and turn the pears over to brown on the other side. Once both the pears and the juices are a medium amber color, remove the pan from the heat and cool for 5 minutes.

Pour the pudding into the prepared pan, then distribute the pears and the caramelized juices evenly over the pudding. Bake in the middle of the oven for 40 to 45 minutes, or until the custard is set and the bread that is popping up between the pears is crispy. Cool for 10 minutes before serving with brandy-spiked Vanilla Sauce.

Storage: This bread pudding is best served the day it is made, but any leftovers can be wrapped in plastic wrap and refrigerated for 2 to 3 days. Rewarm in a 300°F oven for 10 to 15 minutes.

apple crisp with brandy-soaked currants

For the apples in this recipe, we recommend Golden Delicious, Galas, Jonagolds, or any other variety with a high water content (or a combination of varieties), to create an aromatic filling. This recipe calls for soaking dried currants in apple brandy. The longer the currants steep, the more the flavor will be enhanced, so plan accordingly. Our favorite apple brandy, also called *eau de vie*, is made by Steve McCarthy's Clear Creek Distillery (see the Sources section) using Golden Delicious apples grown on the northeast slope of Mt. Hood, just seventy miles east of Portland. The brandy is excellent for both sweet and savory recipes. —*Cory*

┼══ BAKING TIME: 50 MINUTES / SERVES 6 TO 8 ══┼

½ cup (2½ ounces) dried currants

¼ cup apple brandy

1 tablespoon unsalted butter, at room temperature, for pan

CRISP TOPPING

¾ cup packed (5¾ ounces) brown sugar

1¼ cups (6¼ ounces) all-purpose flour

½ teaspoon fine sea salt

1 teaspoon ground cinnamon

½ cup (4 ounces) unsalted butter, melted

FRUIT FILLING

8 large apples, peeled, cored, and sliced ½ inch thick (3 pounds prepped)

¼ cup (1¾ ounces) granulated sugar

2 tablespoons all-purpose flour

Heavy cream, for serving (optional)

Soak the currants in the brandy for at least 2 hours and up to 24 hours.

Preheat the oven to 375°F. Butter a 9-inch square baking pan.

To make the crisp topping, mix the brown sugar, flour, salt, and cinnamon together in a bowl. Stir in the butter, then press the topping together with your hands to form a few small clumps. Put the topping in the freezer while you make the filling.

To make the fruit filling, toss the apples, sugar, and flour together in a bowl until evenly combined, then transfer to the prepared pan.

Scatter the currants and any residual brandy over the apples, then sprinkle the crisp topping evenly over the fruit.

Bake for 50 minutes, or until the crisp is golden and the filling is bubbling up through the topping. Cool for 20 minutes before serving with a drizzle of heavy cream.

Storage: This crisp is best served the day it is made, but any leftovers can be wrapped in plastic wrap and kept at room temperature for 2 to 3 days.

apple pandowdy

A pandowdy recipe can only be altered so much before you leave the wonderful name *pandowdy* behind. The word *dowdy* means unfashionable or without style in appearance. When this pandowdy is served hot from the oven in a cast-iron skillet, it has anything but a dowdy appearance, and it shows great style and flavor when the right apples are chosen. Try a combination of tart and sweet apples to create a perfect balance between texture and juiciness—Northern Spy, Royal Gala, Jonagold, or Cameo, just to name a few. My version of this classic recipe is topped with a rolled biscuit that just barely covers the top of the apples. —*Julie*

BAKING TIME: 35 MINUTES / SERVES 8 TO 12

1 tablespoon unsalted butter, at room temperature, for pan

PASTRY

1½ cups (7½ ounces) all-purpose flour

3 tablespoons granulated sugar

1 teaspoon baking powder

½ teaspoon fine sea salt

6 tablespoons (3 ounces) cold unsalted butter

½ cup cold whole milk, as needed

To make the pastry, mix the flour, sugar, baking powder, and salt together in a bowl. Cut the butter into 1-inch pieces, add to the flour mixture, and toss to evenly coat. Using your fingertips or a pastry blender, cut in the butter until completely broken down into the flour mixture. Add the milk a couple tablespoons at a time, stirring well after each addition to evenly moisten the dough. Add only enough milk for the dough to come together in a relatively dry mass. Gather the dough into a ball, then pat it out into a square. Wrap the dough in plastic wrap and refrigerate while you make the filling.

Preheat the oven to 375°F. Butter a 9-inch cast-iron skillet or 9-inch square baking pan.

FRUIT FILLING

8 large apples, peeled, cored, and each cut into 16 slices (3½ pounds prepped)

⅓ cup (2¼ ounces) granulated sugar

1 teaspoon ground cinnamon

Pinch of fine sea salt

1 tablespoon freshly squeezed lemon juice

1 tablespoon pure vanilla extract

2 tablespoons unsalted butter

Vanilla Bean Ice Cream (page 146), for serving (optional)

To make the fruit filling, toss the apples, sugar, cinnamon, salt, lemon juice, and vanilla together in a large bowl, then transfer the mixture to the prepared pan. Cut the butter into small cubes and scatter over the apples.

Roll out the pastry just a bit smaller than the size of the pan. (The small gap between the pastry and the sides of the pan will allow steam to escape.) Carefully drape the pastry over the apples, then cut 3 steam vents in the pastry.

Bake for 35 minutes, or until the pastry is golden and the filling bubbles up around the edges. This pandowdy is best served warm, topped with a small scoop of Vanilla Bean Ice Cream.

Storage: This pandowdy is best served the day it is made, but any leftovers can be wrapped in plastic and kept at room temperature for 2 to 3 days.

Grandma Freeman's jam cake with brown sugar rum glaze

This recipe hails from my husband's southern-born mother, Betty Kappler. When I asked her if she had any secret baking recipes hidden in her kitchen, she immediately recalled this recipe for jam cake from her grandmother (Grandma Freeman). She even sent me the original recipe, typed on tissue paper, for my collection. Betty recounts that this cake was always waiting for her in the kitchen as a child. Grandma Freeman must have canned a lot of jam in her time, as this recipe requires two cups; it is a great way to use up all that jam that has been forgotten in your refrigerator or to make peace with your overzealous canning last summer. Try a mix of your favorites from tayberry to apricot, or just go with one variety for a more uniform flavor. This cake is very moist and could become an heirloom in your own family. —*Julie*

✤ BAKING TIME: 40 TO 45 MINUTES / SERVES 10 TO 12 ✤

1 tablespoon unsalted butter, at room temperature, for pan

CAKE

2 cups (10 ounces) all-purpose flour

1 teaspoon baking soda

¼ teaspoon fine sea salt

1 teaspoon ground cinnamon

½ teaspoon ground cloves

½ teaspoon freshly grated nutmeg

½ cup (4 ounces) unsalted butter, at room temperature

1 cup (7 ounces) granulated sugar

3 eggs

½ cup buttermilk

2 cups Basic Jam (page 148), or other jam from your pantry

Preheat the oven to 350°F. Butter a 10- to 12-cup Bundt pan.

To make the cake, sift the flour, baking soda, salt, cinnamon, cloves, and nutmeg together in a bowl. Using a handheld mixer with beaters or a stand mixer with the paddle attachment, cream the butter and sugar together on medium-high speed for 3 to 5 minutes, until light and fluffy. Add the eggs one at a time, scraping down the sides of the bowl after each addition. Add half of the flour mixture and mix just until combined, then mix in the buttermilk. Add the remaining flour mixture and mix, again just until combined. Fold in the jam until evenly distributed, but do not overmix. Pour the batter into the prepared pan.

Bake in the middle of the oven for 40 to 45 minutes, or until a wooden skewer inserted into the middle comes out clean and the cake has started to pull away from the sides of the pan. Cool on a wire rack for 20 minutes before inverting the cake onto the cooling rack. Place a baking sheet or some parchment paper under the rack to catch the drips when you glaze the cake.

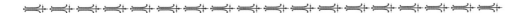

RUM GLAZE

3 tablespoons unsalted butter

½ cup packed (3¾ ounces) brown sugar

¼ cup heavy cream

Pinch of fine sea salt

4 cups (1 pound, 1 ounce) confectioners' sugar

2 tablespoons rum

To make the rum glaze, stir the butter, brown sugar, cream, and salt together in a small saucepan over medium-high heat. Boil the mixture for 5 minutes, stirring occasionally. Sift the confectioners' sugar into a bowl, then pour in the butter mixture and whisk until smooth. Whisk in the rum, then pour the glaze over the cake while it is still slightly warm.

Storage: This cake is a keeper! Wrapped in plastic, it will keep at room temperature for up to 5 days.

pantry

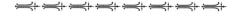

KITCHEN HINT:
Whipping Cream

The key to perfectly whipped cream is to keep it cold and keep your eye on it. Store your cream in the coldest section of the fridge—usually whatever shelf is closest to the freezer. Prechill the bowl and whisk or beaters in the freezer for 10 minutes or so.

If you are using an electric mixer, start whipping the cream on low speed, then gradually increase the speed to medium. We prefer to whip cream by hand because you have much more control over the process. Whipped cream can go from soft to stiff peaks within a matter of strokes, so watch it closely once the whisk starts leaving wakes in the cream. For soft peaks, once the beater starts making tracks in the cream, it is only a matter of moments until the next stage, when the cream holds the faintest of peaks before immediately drooping. You want to reach this precise stage if you are incorporating the cream into other ingredients, as it allows the cream to be whipped a bit further once combined with fruit.

A few more strokes will yield fluffy clouds that mound up and hold their soft shape. This medium stage is what you want as a topping for desserts. If you keep whipping, you will soon hit the stiff peak stage (for those who like to use a fork for their whipped cream). The next stage is on your way to butter—clumpy and grainy. In addition to the cream not tasting so good at this point, your arm will be very tired.

Chantilly cream

Chantilly cream (or crème Chantilly) was made popular by François Vatel, maître d'hotel at the Château du Chantilly in the seventeenth century. Although the name sounds fancy, it is nothing more than sweetened whipped cream. We sweeten ours with sugar and add vanilla. One popular variation also includes brandy. The cream will double in volume when whipped. If possible, do not use ultra-pasteurized heavy cream, as it lacks flavor.

MAKES 2 CUPS

1 cup cold heavy cream

1 teaspoon granulated sugar

½ teaspoon pure vanilla extract

Chill a metal bowl and a whisk. Pour the cream into the bowl and whip with the whisk until soft peaks form. Add the sugar and vanilla and continue whipping the cream until it hangs but does not fall from the whisk. Alternatively, if you are using an electric mixer, start whipping the cream on low speed, then gradually increase the speed until the mixer is on medium speed. (We prefer to whip cream by hand because you have much more control over the process.)

Storage: Chantilly cream is best if served immediately. You may refrigerate it in a covered container for up to 4 hours, but you may need to rewhip some of the cream at the bottom of the bowl before serving.

crème fraîche

Crème fraîche is easy to make at home, if you have the time. Avoid ultra-pasteurized whipping cream for this recipe, as it lacks flavor.

MAKES ABOUT 1 CUP

1 cup cold heavy cream

2 tablespoons buttermilk

Heat the cream until steaming but not boiling, then stir in the buttermilk. Transfer the mixture to a clean bowl, partially cover, and let sit at room temperature (preferably in a warm room) for 24 to 36 hours. (Do not fret that the cream will go bad; the buttermilk prevents any bad bacteria from forming.) Stir and taste the cream every 6 hours or so. As it ages, it will thicken. It is ready when it has the consistency of very thick cream and a nutty, tangy flavor. Cover and chill in the refrigerator, where it will continue to thicken a bit as it ages.

Storage: Stored in an airtight container, crème fraîche will keep in the refrigerator for up to 7 days.

vanilla bean ice cream

Homemade ice cream is always such a treat! This ice cream tastes much better if you use a real vanilla bean. If you do not have one, you can add a tablespoon of pure vanilla extract when you stir in the cream at the end.

MAKES 4 CUPS

Seeds scraped from ½ vanilla bean

3 cups half-and-half

1 cup (7 ounces) granulated sugar

6 egg yolks

⅛ teaspoon fine sea salt

½ cup heavy cream

Put the vanilla bean seeds into a 3-quart saucepan, then add the half-and-half, ½ cup of the sugar, and the vanilla bean pod and place over medium-low heat. Cook, stirring occasionally, just until warm.

Separately, whisk the yolks, the remaining ½ cup sugar, and the salt together in a bowl. Continue whisking until slightly thickened and lighter in color. Slowly pour half of the warm vanilla mixture into the egg yolks, whisking continuously. Next, pour the yolk mixture back into the saucepan and cook over medium heat, stirring constantly, until the mixture thickens and coats the back of a spoon.

Set a bowl over an ice bath, then strain the custard through a fine-mesh sieve set over the bowl. Remove and discard the vanilla bean pod.

Stir in the cream and continue stirring until cool, then cover and refrigerate for about 2 hours, until completely chilled.

Freeze in an ice-cream maker according to the manufacturer's directions. Place the churned ice cream in a dry plastic container and cover with plastic wrap directly on top of the ice cream. Chill for at least 2 hours, until set up, before serving.

Storage: Stored in an airtight container in the freezer, the ice cream will keep for up to 2 weeks (as if!).

berry ice cream

Berry ice cream is a summertime delight. For this recipe, just about any variety of berry will work. It is important to chop the fruit into small pieces. If the pieces are too big, they will become hard, clumpy ice crystals. On the other hand, if you mash the fruit up too much, you may end up with an essentially smooth ice cream, without flavorful bits of fruit in the finished product. Somewhere in between is perfect.

MAKES 4 CUPS

2 cups whole milk

1 cup heavy cream

1 cup (7 ounces) granulated sugar

4 egg yolks

Pinch of fine sea salt

2 teaspoons pure vanilla extract

1 dry pint (2 cups) berries, finely chopped

Combine the milk, $1/2$ cup of the cream, and $1/3$ cup of the sugar in a 3-quart sauce-pan over medium-low heat and cook, stirring occasionally, just until warm.

Separately, whisk together the yolks, $1/3$ cup of the remaining sugar, and the salt and continue whisking until slightly thickened and lighter in color. Slowly pour half of the warmed liquid into the yolk mixture, whisk-ing continuously. Next, pour the yolk mixture back into the saucepan and cook over medium heat, stirring constantly, until the mixture thickens and coats the back of a spoon.

CONTINUED

Set a bowl over an ice bath, then strain the custard through a fine-mesh sieve set over the bowl. Stir in the remaining $1/2$ cup cream and the vanilla and continue stirring until cool, then cover and refrigerate for about 2 hours, until completely chilled.

At the same time you put the custard in the refrigerator, add the remaining $1/3$ cup sugar to the berries and refrigerate until the custard is chilled.

Stir the berries into the custard and freeze in an ice-cream maker according to the manufacturer's directions. Place the churned ice cream in a dry plastic container and cover with plastic wrap directly on top of the ice cream. Chill for at least 2 hours, until set up, before serving.

Storage: Stored in an airtight container in the freezer, the ice cream will keep for up to 2 weeks.

basic jam

Jam is fun and easy to make. It is best to make it in small batches, so the jam can come to a boil quickly. The shorter the amount of time the jam is on the stove, the more it will taste like fruit and not syrup. The amount of sugar you add to the fruit is variable, depending on the sweetness or tartness of the fruit. Jam makers disagree on how much sugar to use; while one home canner I know swears that jam should be 65 percent sugar (counting the natural sugar in the fruit), another tells me she adds as little as 20 percent sugar to her jam. Both of their jams are wonder-

ful, which only goes to show that you should always taste the fruit before you add the sugar. —*Cory*

MAKES 3 TO 4 CUPS

4 cups chopped fruit (about 2 pounds)

3 cups (1 pound, 5 ounces) granulated sugar, as needed

Juice of 1 lemon

Put the fruit, sugar, and lemon juice in a large, heavy saucepan and cook over high heat, stirring occasionally to avoid any burning on the bottom of the pan. Skim off any foam that gathers on the surface. The jam should boil for at least 5 minutes. To set, the jam must reach 221°F. If you do not have a candy thermometer, you can test the jam by putting a few drops onto a plate that has been chilled in the freezer; you will quickly be able to see how runny the finished jam will be once it is on the cold plate. Once the jam thickens to the desired consistency, remove from the heat.

Storage: Stored in a clean, sealed glass jar in the refrigerator, the jam will keep for a few weeks. Alternatively, you can process the jam following instructions for home canning.

vanilla sauce

This sauce is the American version of crème anglaise, a vanilla custard sauce. Our recipe makes a basic vanilla sauce that goes well with every dessert. To enhance the sauce, you can add liquor (Calvados or pear brandy comes to mind). This sauce does not require heavy cream to taste sinful. Here, we use a milk base to create a simple, decadent sauce.

MAKES 1½ CUPS

1 cup whole milk

4 egg yolks

⅓ cup (2¼ ounces) granulated sugar

⅛ teaspoon fine sea salt

1 teaspoon pure vanilla extract

2 to 4 tablespoons liquor (optional)

Heat the milk in a 2-quart saucepan over medium-low heat just until warm. In a bowl, whisk together the yolks, sugar, and salt until slightly thickened and lighter in color. Slowly pour half of the warm milk into the yolk mixture, whisking continuously. Next, pour the yolk mixture back into the saucepan and cook over medium heat, stirring constantly, until the mixture thickens and thickly coats the back of a spoon.

Set a bowl over an ice bath, then strain the custard through a fine-mesh sieve set over the bowl. Add the vanilla and stir until cool. Stir in liquor to taste, then refrigerate for about 2 hours, until completely chilled, before serving.

Storage: Stored in an airtight container, vanilla sauce will keep in the refrigerator for up to 5 days.

vanilla crumb

This crumb topping can be used on many recipes because it is so versatile. With a little customizing of this recipe, you can make a topping for any fruit crisp. Double or even triple the recipe and keep the extra topping in the freezer; that way, you can make a crisp on the spur of the moment.

MAKES 2 CUPS

1 cup (5 ounces) all-purpose flour

¾ cup (5¼ ounces) granulated sugar

¼ cup packed (1⅞ ounces) light brown sugar

¼ teaspoon fine sea salt

½ cup (4 ounces) cold unsalted butter, cut into ¼-inch cubes

1 tablespoon pure vanilla extract

Combine the flour, sugars, salt, and butter in the bowl of a food processor or a stand mixer with the paddle attachment. If using a food processor, pulse until the mixture is the texture of coarse crumbs. With a stand mixer, combine on low speed, also until the texture of coarse crumbs. Drizzle the vanilla over the mixture and either pulse or mix briefly to distribute the vanilla.

Storage: Use this topping immediately, or store it in a plastic bag in the freezer for up to 3 months.

Three Tips for Perfection

Before you add sugar to the fruit, taste it. Is the fruit sweet? Tart? Somewhere in between? If the fruit is very tart, you may want to add more sugar than the recipe calls for. If it is sweet, you could cut back on the sugar. If you are not sure whether to add more or less sugar, start with less than the recipe calls for and work your way up. Let the sugared fruit sit for about 10 minutes, then taste again to decide if you should add more sugar.

Always let pastry dough rest after rolling. This reduces shrinkage during baking and will ensure the crust is the proper size.

Consider using a pie crust shield to prevent the edges of the crust from overbrowning. A pie crust shield is a ring commonly made of aluminum or silicon. You can also devise one yourself using aluminum foil. Placed gently over the pie halfway through the baking process, the shield shelters the crust from the oven's heat and prevents overbrowning.

Tips for Perfect Pie Crust

Making pie pastry can be quick and easy if you follow a few basic guidelines:

Keep everything cold. If at any time during the process your ingredients warm up, simply place the ingredients (or the dough itself) in the refrigerator until cool.

Use an acid (such as lemon juice) to help prevent tough dough.

Use all-purpose or pastry flour.

Look for European-style butter, which has a higher butterfat content and lower moisture, for optimum flavor and flakiness.

The final dough should have visible pieces of butter the size of small peas in order to achieve flaky results. The butter is trapped between the dough structures, and when it melts from the heat of the oven, steam is created. This process creates the flakiness of a good pie crust.

Chilling the dough for at least 30 minutes (preferably an hour) allows the dough to relax and the butter to chill out. You will benefit from this rest, too, as you will have an easier time rolling out the dough and a flakier crust in the end.

Practice makes perfect! The more you make pastry, the more you will develop a feel for the process.

all-butter pie pastry

There are many ways to make pie dough, but in all instances it is essentially a combination of flour, fat, and liquid. Different recipes call for different fats—typically, shortening, lard or butter, or some combination thereof. In our experience, an all-butter crust is tried-and-true. Butter has wonderful flavor, and it works well in pastry crusts if you treat it properly, as described below. One important step to achieving a tasty, flaky crust is to start with cold ingredients. Also, do not overwork the dough. Always be patient and let it rest. Because the dough keeps well in the freezer for up to 3 months, we provide a recipe that will make enough for four 9-inch single-crust pies or two double-crust pies.

MAKES FOUR 9-INCH PIE SHELLS

5 cups (1 pound, 9 ounces) all-purpose flour

3 tablespoons granulated sugar

1½ teaspoons fine sea salt

2 cups (1 pound) cold unsalted butter

1 cup ice water, or more as needed

2 tablespoons freshly squeezed lemon juice (about ½ lemon)

Put the flour, sugar, and salt in a bowl, stir to combine, then put the bowl in the freezer for about 10 minutes, until super cold.

Cut the butter into 1-inch cubes, then add it to the flour mixture and toss to evenly coat. Cut the butter into the flour mixture using a pastry blender, food processor, electric mixer, or your hands, just until the mixture becomes coarse and crumbly and the butter is about the size of peas.

Stir the water and lemon juice together, then drizzle over the dry ingredients, 1/3 cup at a time, tossing with a fork to distribute the liquid. The pastry will be shaggy but should hold together when squeezed in the palm of your hand; if not, add an additional teaspoon or two of ice water.

Dump the pastry onto a lightly floured work surface and press down on the dough, folding it over on itself a few times until it holds together. Try not to handle it too much, or it will warm up and may become overdeveloped. Divide the pastry into 4 equal parts and shape each piece into a disk 1 inch thick. Wrap each disk in plastic wrap and chill for 1 hour.

To roll out the pastry, see the tips on page 152.

Storage: If wrapped well, the disks will keep for up to 3 days in the refrigerator, or up to 3 months in the freezer. Defrost frozen disks in the refrigerator overnight.

Tips for Rolling Out Pastry for Pie Crusts and Tart Shells

Roll out the dough with the smallest amount of flour possible. At Baker & Spice, we use rice flour when rolling out dough because it is not absorbed into pastry dough and it creates a sandy surface that prevents sticking.

Begin in the center of the disk and, using even pressure, roll the dough out toward the edge, turning the dough every few strokes to shape a circle and prevent the dough from sticking. It is a good idea to flip the dough over and roll it on the other side, too. This helps to keep both sides smooth and also helps to prevent sticking.

For ease of lining the pan, roll the pastry out a bit larger than the pan. Trim any excess dough with a knife. Dock the pastry with a fork. This helps to prevent shrinkage during baking.

Once the dough is in the pan, let it rest. Chill the crust for 30 to 60 minutes to relax the dough.

When rolling out scraps of pie dough, stack them on top of each other rather than kneading them together. This helps create flaky layers. Wrap any scraps of dough in plastic wrap and store them in the refrigerator in case you need to fix any cracks.

short dough

When making this recipe, keep in mind that the dough needs to rest both before and after it is rolled out. This will ease the rolling process and prevent the crust from shrinking once it is in the oven.

MAKES ONE 10-INCH TART SHELL

1½ cups (7½ ounces) all-purpose flour

¼ cup (1¾ ounces) granulated sugar

¼ teaspoon fine sea salt

½ cup (4 ounces) cold unsalted butter, cut into ¼-inch cubes

2 tablespoons heavy cream

1 egg yolk

Put the flour, sugar, and salt in a bowl and stir to combine. Add the butter and, using either your hands, a pastry blender, an electric mixer, or a food processor, work the butter into the flour mixture until it resembles coarse cornmeal. Lightly beat the cream and egg yolk together, then stir into the flour mixture with a fork. Mix just until the dough is blended and comes together into one mass. Form the dough into a 6-inch disk, wrap in plastic wrap, and refrigerate for 1 hour.

To roll the dough out for a 10-inch tart pan, place the disk on a lightly floured surface and, using even pressure, roll out toward the edge, turning the dough every few strokes to shape a circle and prevent the dough from sticking. Roll the dough into a 12-inch circle about ⅛ inch thick.

CONTINUED

To prebake the tart shell before filling, see the tips on this page.

Storage: If wrapped well, the disk will keep for up to 3 days in the refrigerator, or up to 3 months in the freezer. Defrost the frozen disk in the refrigerator overnight.

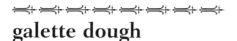

galette dough

For a galette, you need your dough to be a tad stronger than for a pie because there is no pan to support the filling. If the dough has any weak points, the filling is sure to find them and ooze out all around the galette. Any leaking juices have the potential to burn. To prevent this from happening, a good galette dough incorporates the butter further into the flour than a typical pie dough. This process creates a dough that is less flaky but noticeably sturdier.

MAKES ONE 10-INCH GALETTE CRUST

1¾ cups (8¾ ounces) all-purpose flour

1 tablespoon granulated sugar

¾ teaspoon fine sea salt

¾ cup (6 ounces) cold unsalted butter

3 tablespoons ice water, or more as needed

1 teaspoon freshly squeezed lemon juice

Put the flour, sugar, and salt in a bowl, stir to combine, then put the bowl in the freezer for about 10 minutes, until super cold.

Cut the butter into ½-inch cubes, then add it to the flour mixture and toss until each cube of butter is coated with the flour mixture. Cut

CONTINUED

KITCHEN HINT:

Prebaking a Crust

To prebake (aka blind bake) a pie or tart crust:

Preheat the oven to 375°F.

Line the pan with the rolled-out pastry, then lay a piece of parchment paper, aluminum foil, or a large coffee filter over the pastry; it should be large enough to completely cover the crust, including the sides. Fill the pan with commercial pie weights, dried beans, or uncooked rice, and spread the weights out to the edge of the pan, building them up toward the sides to support the sides during baking. Set the pan on a baking sheet (which will make it easy to move the pan to and from the oven) and bake in the middle of the oven for 35 to 40 minutes.

Remove the crust from the oven, leaving the oven on, and remove the weights by slowly lifting the parchment paper out of the crust. Return the crust to the oven for an additional 10 to 15 minutes, until the pastry is lightly golden.

Once the crust has cooled, look for cracks. It is important to fix any cracks; otherwise, the filling could ooze out and make a mess. Repair any cracks with leftover uncooked dough, gently pressing or smearing the dough into the crevices before pouring the filling into the crust.

Storage: A crust can be prebaked one day in advance. Wrap the cooled shell in plastic wrap and store at room temperature.

the butter into the flour using a pastry blender, food processor, electric mixer, or your hands, just until the ingredients become coarse and crumbly and the butter is slightly smaller than a pea.

Stir the water and lemon juice together, then drizzle over the dough, tossing with a fork to distribute the liquid. The pastry will be shaggy but should hold together when squeezed in the palm of your hand; if not, add an additional teaspoon or two of ice water.

Dump the pastry onto a lightly floured work surface and press down on the dough, folding it over on itself a few times until it holds together. Try not to handle it too much, or it will get warm and may become overdeveloped. Flatten the pastry out into a disk approximately 1 inch thick. Wrap in plastic wrap and chill for 1 hour.

Storage: If wrapped well, the disk will keep for up to 3 days in the refrigerator, or up to 3 months in the freezer. Defrost the frozen dough in the refrigerator overnight.

vanilla bean shortbread

Shortbread cookies are a mainstay at Baker & Spice. They are a perfect complement to the rich taste of stewed fruit, and when crushed, they can also be used as a crust for desserts.

BAKING TIME: 18 TO 20 MINUTES
MAKES 48 COOKIES

⅓ cup (2¼ ounces) granulated sugar

Seeds scraped from ½ vanilla bean

2 cups (1 pound) unsalted butter, at room temperature

1¼ cups (6 ounces) unsifted confectioners' sugar

¾ teaspoon fine sea salt

2 teaspoons pure vanilla extract

3¾ cups (1 pound, 2¾ ounces) all-purpose flour

½ cup (2½ ounces) rice flour

1 egg white, beaten

½ cup (4 ounces) turbinado sugar

Stir the granulated sugar and vanilla bean seeds together in the bowl of an upright mixer with the paddle attachment, then add the butter, confectioners' sugar, and salt and mix on medium speed for 1 to 2 minutes, until fully incorporated but not light and fluffy. Stir in the vanilla and scrape down the sides of the bowl. Stir in the flours in two additions, scraping down the bowl after each addition. Fully incorporate the flour without overmixing.

Dump the mixture onto a work surface and divide it into two pieces. Place each on a piece of parchment paper measuring 12 by 16 inches. Shape each piece of dough into a log about 12 inches long, then fold the parchment over the dough and roll the log back and forth. The parchment paper will help to smooth out the dough and keep the log an even diameter. Transfer both logs to a baking sheet and refrigerate for about 2 hours, until firm.

Preheat the oven to 350°F.

With a pastry brush, coat each log with the egg white, then roll the logs in the turbinado sugar. Slice each log ½ inch thick and arrange the cookies on a baking sheet 1 inch apart. Bake for 18 to 20 minutes, or until the edges

CONTINUED

are golden brown and the cookies are firm in the center. Allow to cool before enjoying.

Storage: Stored in an airtight container at room temperature, the shortbread will keep for about 7 days. You can also freeze the unbaked logs, well wrapped, for up to 2 months.

vanilla chiffon cake

Chiffon cake is light and lovely, whether served on its own, with fresh berries, or as the base of a trifle. The consistency of the beaten egg whites is crucial for optimum texture of the cake.

BAKING TIME: 35 MINUTES
MAKES ONE 9-INCH CAKE

1 tablespoon unsalted butter, at room temperature, for pan

2 cups sifted (7½ ounces) cake flour

1½ teaspoons baking powder

¼ teaspoon fine sea salt

6 tablespoons (3 ounces) unsalted butter, at room temperature

¾ cup plus ⅓ cup (5¼ ounces plus 2¼ ounces) granulated sugar

1 tablespoon pure vanilla extract

¾ cup plus 2 tablespoons tepid water

3 egg whites

Preheat the oven to 350°F. Lightly butter a 9-inch by 2-inch round baking pan.

Sift the flour, baking powder, and salt together two times in a bowl. Using a hand-held mixer with beaters or a stand mixer with the paddle attachment, cream the butter and ¾ cup sugar on medium-high speed for 3 to 5 minutes, until light and fluffy, then blend in the vanilla. Stir in the flour mixture in three additions alternating with the water in two additions, starting and ending with the flour mixture and scraping down the sides of the bowl occasionally.

In a separate, clean bowl of an electric mixer, whisk the egg whites until soft peaks form. Slowly add ⅓ cup sugar in a steady stream and beat on medium-high speed until the whites hold firm and shiny peaks. Using a rubber spatula, gently fold one-third of the whites into the batter to loosen its consistency, then fold in the remaining whites just until incorporated.

Pour the batter into the prepared pan and bake in the middle of the oven for 35 minutes, or until the cake pulls slightly away from the sides of the pan and becomes firm on top. Cool on a wire rack for 20 minutes, then remove the cake from the pan.

Storage: Covered with plastic wrap, the cake can be stored at room temperature for 1 to 2 days, or in the freezer for up to 1 month.

Whipping Egg Whites

Before you start, make sure your bowl and utensils are clean, free of any grease or soap, and completely dry.

For ease of separation, divide eggs while they are cold, but then allow the whites to come to room temperature for best whipping performance. If you want to speed the process, you can set the container of whites in a bowl of warm water and stir until they are at room temperature.

Egg whites triple in volume when whipped properly, so choose your bowl size wisely. Copper or stainless steel is best, and definitely steer away from plastic; you never know what fat particles are hiding in the pores.

Use an electric mixer or a big balloon whisk to make the process go more quickly, and add a pinch of salt to help break down the gelatinous consistency of the whites.

When whipping egg whites without sugar (like when folding them into batter), whip them just until they start holding shape. When you pull the whisk from the bowl, you should have soft, shiny peaks that look moist and fall over slightly. Whites whipped without sugar are weaker than those with sugar. Continue whipping a bit further for stiff peaks. One trick is that less is always more. You will know you have gone too far if the whites appear lumpy and dry.

When whipping whites with sugar (as for a meringue), you have a bit more control over the process. Whip the whites just to the soft peak stage before adding the sugar, then add the sugar slowly in a steady stream while whipping, and continue whipping until you reach the desired stage. Sugar acts like a liquid when added to whites, so you want to get a head start on the whites before introducing the sugar. The larger the amount of sugar added, the stiffer and more stable the whites will be.

Sources

Your local farmers market: www.localharvest.org (nationwide link)

Andy's Orchard (www.andysorchard.com): a wide variety of dried fruit from California

Bob's Red Mill (www.bobsredmill.com): dry goods, flours, and spices

Cherry Country (www.thecherrycountry.com): dried organic cherries—both tart and sweet—from Oregon

Clear Creek Distillery (www.clearcreekdistillery.com): apple and pear brandy, as well as other eaux-de-vie, made at a distillery in Portland, Oregon

Freddy Guys Hazelnuts (www.freddyguys.com): hazelnuts from Oregon

Glenmore Farms (www.glenmorefarms.com): jams and syrups from Oregon

King Arthur (www.kingarthurflour.com): flours, pans, and specialty ingredients for bakers

Mandelin (www.mandelininc.com): natural almonds and almond paste from California

Omega Farm: (www.omegafarm.com): organic Bartlett pears from Washington

Penzeys Spices (www.penzeys.com): a wide variety of spices from around the world

Sweetwares (www.sweetwares.com): fine baking supplies, ingredients, and instruction

Index